From Trenches to Triumph...

Overcoming yourself and others

By Dave Clark

From Trenches to Triumph...

Overcoming yourself and others

Copyright © 2017 by Dave Clark

Neither the publisher nor the author can be held responsible for the reader's ultimate degree of success. As in any business it is the reader's responsibility to know, understand, and follow all applicable tax and real estate laws in their area, from the purchase to the repair, rental, or sale of the property. All rights reserved. No portion of this publication may be reproduced, stored in a retrieval system, or transmitted by any means—electronic, mechanical, photocopying, recording, or any other—except for brief quotations in printed reviews, without the prior written permission of the publisher.

Cover Design: Amy Vega

Interior Design: 3-Sixty Design Studio

Indigo River Publishing
3 West Garden Street Ste. 352
Pensacola, FL 32502
www.indigoriverpublishing.com

Ordering Information:

Quantity sales: Special discounts are available on quantity purchases by corporations, associations, and others. For details, contact the publisher at the address above.

Orders by U.S. trade bookstores and wholesalers: Please contact the publisher at the address above.

Printed in the United States of America

Library of Congress Control Number: 2017940459

ISBN: 978-0-9972945-9-0

First Edition

With Indigo River Publishing, you can always expect great books, strong voices, and meaningful messages. Most importantly, you'll always find...words worth reading.

Table of Contents

Chapter 1 Defining moment, establishing credibility, presenting dilemma/challenge 7

Chapter 2 Overcoming fears, making choices and goals, continuing to establish credibility 21

Chapter 3 Vision comes before the plan 33

Chapter 4 Education can come from different venues 49

Chapter 5 Know your craft 59

Chapter 6 Implementing Your Plan 71

Chapter 7 Dealing with Failure 85

Chapter 8 Building a Team...101

The last chapter! Closing..127

Foreword

Sales is the lifeblood of every company and becoming a professional salesman can be the highest of paid professions. David Clark understands this better than most. As a seasoned entrepreneur and investor myself, I look at many deals and commonly come across opportunities to collaborate or joint venture with others.

There are so many entrepreneurs, or in many cases wannapreneurs, that will talk about the size of their market or field, potential market share capture, and scalability. They have become proficient in many aspects of business, but shy away from personally taking part in the sales arm of the company. This is where all of the action is and anyone who hasn't learned to love the game of sales hasn't developed the right skillsets. They are also most likely unable to properly manage their fear.

Successful people in many ways learn to become comfortable with discomfort and have learned to love sales. Dave Clark truly loves the game of sales and has become a masterful teacher and mentor to thousands. I met Dave several years ago through a mutual friend and within five minutes I knew we were cut from the same cloth. Since that time we have collaborated on numerous projects and have shared the stage on many occasions.

When I was honing my skills as a young businessman and learning the art of sales, I quickly learned that I had to invest in myself to get the return I was looking for. It was common for me to go through five to six books per month, so I could learn from others that were clearly at the top of the sales game. Over the years, the stigma of sales has changed and a few shady characters have burned bridges for many. The result? Over the last two decades there are very few that have aspired to be the Nation's next great salesman. In fact, if you introduce yourself as a salesman, many people would shy away or have preconceived ideas as to your character. This has caused a huge problem! Since most of the greats are up in age or have come to pass, and very few were left to fill their shoes, we are now faced with a dilemma: the great salesman is close to extinction. Today, there is everything from small businesses to multi-million dollar corporations that have little to no sales departments, and the people running these departments are missing even the most basic of fundamentals. The person that embraces the game of sales and learns how to master it, truly has the world as their oyster.

I believe that when you mention the greats like Dale Carnegie, Zig Ziglar, Brian Tracy, or Tom Hopkins, David Clark's name should definitely be included. His understanding of sales, combined with his ability to befriend anyone and a work ethic that is bar none, David Clark is a person that you will want to get to know. I strong urge you to read this book in its entirety, and to apply what David has put together for over five decades. I am fortunate to have him as an alliance and honored to have him as a friend.

Dan Vega – Entrepreneur, Speaker, Investor

CHAPTER 1

Defining moment, establishing credibility, presenting dilemma/challenge

From Trenches to Triumph...

Many Americans today are grappling with life-changing events that affect not only their livelihoods but also the lives of ones who are dependent on them. Military personnel who are transitioning to civilian society, employees who have lost their jobs to outsourcing or downsizing, ambitious individuals who are stuck in boring, dead-end jobs, and others who are forced into retirement are all desperately searching for new careers and means to earn a living. Most will be confronted with intense soul searching and will be forced to make difficult personal decisions regarding uncertain futures. Over the years, my own personal business experiences have compelled me to look inward and make difficult professional choices time and time again. In this book, I will lay bare my mistakes and successes, and share information, guidance, tips, case studies, and personal stories that will help the reader plot a path to a new and prosperous career.

I think that you know at an early age if you are going to be someone who is more than just a follower or a mindless robot. What I mean by that statement is the following: are you going to make your own way in life or are you always going to depend on others to set your path in life? I decided at the age of nine that owning my own business was far better than doing all the work for someone else and receiving few of the rewards. I asked my dad questions about starting

Chapter One

my own business. When I was only nine, he sent me to sell peanuts with my first cousin in Gainesville, Florida. We sold each bag of peanuts for ten cents. I would make three cents for every bag of peanuts that I had sold. This was my first experience in sales, and I knew that I had found my new passion. My territory included small businesses and the court house. I met a lot of interesting people this way. The District Judge McDonald, the local sheriff, and the local newspaper staff were some of my customers. I developed many long-lasting friends with these individuals. It was a wonderful time for me because I now had older folks as friends and mentors.

It was not easy for me to establish a route for sales. At first, I was scared to go up to people and ask them to buy a bag of peanuts. Sometimes, I would stand on the street corner and call out "Boiled Peanuts!" and hope someone would come over and buy them. I had to get up the nerve to enter a business and then ask the employees if they wanted to buy some peanuts. I remember being so scared and feeling so small. I was very small for my age. The best motivator for me was fear. I knew if I didn't sell the peanuts I was given, I would lose my job. Even though I worked for my cousin, he could easily replace me. He was in the business to make money, not to give family favors by keeping someone who wouldn't work.

My parents were just like everybody else struggling to make ends meet. We never had extra money. So, for me to have a job that gave me spending money was great! It felt really good to be able to do things, like go to the movies on Saturday mornings. It felt even better knowing that I was paying for myself (It's a shame to see kids today who think that they deserve to have everything they want materially without earning the money to pay for it. They are the entitlement generation). I loved having an entrepreneurial spirit.

After a while, I started questioning why I was working for my cousin. What kind of money could I make if I owned the peanut business? My dad explained to me that my cousin was making four cents per bag of peanuts when I was making only three cents per bag of peanuts. It didn't take an Einstein moment to reach a conclusion on the matter. Immediately, I wanted to start my own business so that I could make twice as much as an owner rather than a salesperson. You might have felt this way too. If you have, then you are reading the right book. Not everybody wants to work for themselves or own a company, but you can do it if you are willing to commit to your goal and pay the price.

My dad was not as much of a risk taker as I was. He was good father who taught me honor, integrity, and honesty. However, my dad did not allow me to go into business for myself. The difference between my dad and me was that he

Chapter One

was happy working for others, and I wanted more. So the desire to have my own company or do what I love has been my own journey.

My Defining Moment

Think back to when you were forced to make a decision. You had a choice. You either accepted the choice that was made for you or you made your own decision.

When I was in the third grade I thought that I was a good student until one day in reading class my teacher had an open reading session. She separated the class into the best readers, the good readers, and the slow readers. Each student had to read a paragraph from the book so that the teacher knew which group to assign. When I read before the whole class, it became apparent that I was not a good reader. She stopped me, pointed to the slow readers group and told me that I would be in that group. I was horrified because the other students looked down on the slow readers and called them the "stupid group."

When the bell rang, I went home feeling stupid. I decided right then that no one, not even I, was going to call me stupid. When I got home, my mom was busy doing the dishes and I asked her to read a portion of the book to me.

From Trenches to Triumph...

Now, my tenacity and will to win kicked in. I looked at each word she read and formed the sentences in my head. As she read, I engraved the words in my brain. When she was done, I took the book and went to my room and read the story over and over again until I fell asleep knowing how to read the book.

The next day in reading class, the teacher put the students in their respective groups. When she asked for a reader, I was the first one to raise my hand. She was a little taken aback. There I was in the stupid group, and I wanted to read first.

She said, "Ok."

I stood and read the book like a scholar.

She was so amazed. She said "I made a mistake; you're in the wrong group. You belong in the best reading group!"

I immediately got my things and ran to my new group. I had done it and vowed it would never happen to me again.

As I think back on my formative years, I can distinctly recollect another experience that could be classified as a "defining moment." The year was 1960. I was in the seventh grade, and my parents had just gotten a divorce. As a

Chapter One

result, I went to live with my father at his sister's farm in Alabama. My father was out of work and planned to leave for California to work in construction. He left me with my Aunt Lessie, and she became like a second mother to me. Although she loved me, she had a very large farm that needed to be tended to. So she put me to work in the cotton fields. I didn't mind working on the farm because it was my way of paying for my room and board. I didn't how long I would be staying with her while my dad was in California, so I worked hard to earn my keep.

If you know anything about Alabama in the summertime, you know that it is hot and humid. My aunt was in her sixties and could pick cotton faster than anyone I knew. I was a young boy, and she could pick more cotton than I could. One day, I was picking in the fields, and it must've been nearly a hundred degrees with high humidity. Because of the way the fields were set up, the drinking water was at the end of each row. You had to pick an entire row before you could get a sip. My hands were raw and bloody from the burs, and my back hurt from constantly bending over; I was hot, sweaty, tired, and thirsty. I looked up to the heavens and said, "There has to be a better way to earning a living than this." One day, this farm could be my future. Following in my family's footsteps would offer only what I saw that day. I said, "If I get out of this cotton field alive, I will never come back." I knew, that day, that I would make a better life for me.

From Trenches to Triumph...

I stayed with my aunt for the rest of the summer until my father sent for my brother and me. I finished high school in San Lorenzo, CA and decided not to attend college. I was tired of school and wanted to enjoy being young. I worked and enjoyed the break. When I did go to college, I met my first wife and married. Upon applying for college, I was drafted and spent the next three years in the military service.

After I got out of the army in 1971, I went back to the job I had when I was drafted. I worked for Safeway. It was a good job and had excellent benefits. I worked hard and could have started a career with Safeway. I enjoyed the work, but the management was not reliable. I never understood how the assistant managers gained their position. The general manager knew his job well. I respected and liked him. The assistant managers would drive me crazy. No matter how hard I worked, it seemed that the ones who didn't do their job well were the ones who moved ahead. This reminded me of how I felt when I was nine years old in the peanut business. After several years at Safeway, I decided to venture out on my own.

I went into construction and loved it. The more I did, the more I would get paid. I worked "piece work" which is pay equal to effort. After the oil crunch, jobs in construction dried up quickly as situations similar to today. Here I again

Chapter One

faced a decision to change my profession. I desired to be my own boss. So I went into the automotive striping business. I was in one of the first training classes for Trim-Line. I borrowed money from a friend for the initial start-up cost. My new company would take me to Colorado. Just before we left California, I received my first credit card. It had a four hundred dollar limit. I used three hundred and fifty dollars of the credit card to move. It cost me a hundred dollars in gas which left me with about a hundred dollars in the bank, so I did not have enough money to return to California. I had a wife and a one-year-old son. I also had a car payment, owed a friend fifteen hundred dollars, and needed to pay rent and utilities. On my first day, I stood staring at my car and thought about how I need a truck instead. I was terrified. I had to make it, my family depended on me. I could feel my legs shaking. My life-long dream became a reality and hit me. I had to make it or lose everything.

Not having any friends yet, I turned to the one person who's always there for me. I said a big long prayer to God. I got in my car and headed for Boulder, Colorado. I drove straight to the Datsun Dealer, which is now Nissan. I worked up the courage to ask for the sales manager. When the owner came out, I introduced myself to him and showed him some pictures of my striping. I told him that I would do one side of the first car for free. If he didn't like it, I would take it off. If he liked it, I would stripe the other side, and that side would cost him. He agreed.

He loved it. He gestured to his lot and said, "Go do those ten cars." I worked there most of the day. He gave me more cars to stripe. At the end of the day, I had earned over three hundred dollars. I had never earned that kind of money before. I had told my wife if I made a hundred dollars that day we could go out to a steak dinner. I wanted her to feel safe and secure. I didn't want her to worry. I was earning enough for both of us. After I rushed home, I hugged and kissed my wife and told her we were going out for steak. By the end of the week, we had gone out for steak four times. I was able to pay off my credit card, pay my friend back, and, after three months, buy a new Datsun truck and new car. My hard work proved that self-employment could lead to success.

My career in automobile striping lasted ten years but ended when I was in a horrible automobile accident which injured my neck, knee, and back. The healing process was slow and agonizing. Every day it was a chore to get out of bed. I had to roll onto the floor, crawl to the wall, and lean on it to stand. Even through the pain, I continued to stripe cars and never missed a day of work. I knew that I couldn't keep the same pace as before and that it was time for another change.

Chapter One

I reasoned that sales was a less physically demanding job. I had heard about an opportunity selling fire alarms for homes. The job required a small up-front cost for inventory, but this time, I had to sell from door to door.

If I bought sixty alarms a month, I would receive six alarms for free. If you have ever done door-to-door, you know how hard it is. You are alone everyday, doing the same thing over and over again. You start to talk to yourself often. I became so good at sales that I usually sold all the alarms that I bought. I was able to support my family with the lifestyle I wanted. I was glad that I had learned to overcome my fear of approaching people when I was ten years old selling peanuts. You have to face your fears head on. Door-to-door sales was similar to selling peanuts: the more I did it, the easier it became.

I am still in sales and have been selling cookware for over thirty years. I love the product and what it can do for people. As I look back on the choices I have made in business, I am grateful that I didn't let others make my decisions for me

Not everybody will face the same challenges that I had. If you want to advance in your profession or start and new one, go for it! I did, and I would not trade anything for that time of my life. I like the saying from Gary Coxe's book. It says, "Don't let others rent space in your mind." In other words, you put ideas to work in your head. Even close family members think they are doing you a favor by telling you not to do this or that. I wanted to determine my own future. Failure would not be the end of the world. I would just find another way to accomplish my goal.

Take your dream and ask yourself, "What am I waiting for?" The fear of failure may be what is stopping you. Failure is a learning experience that shows you how to do things better. You should never quit on your dream or vision. If I can do it, so can you. Take the time to lay out your vision. Do not listen to people who give advice on something they know nothing about. You can succeed if you want it bad enough and are willing to pay the price.

As you read this book, take time to reflect on your "defining moment." We all have one. It makes you who you are today. You might have to think about it for a while, but there is one. Write it down and read it back to yourself. You are learning who you are and what you can do to become even better. Now, you know what to work on. This is your life and your decision. Make a good choice, and you will reach your vision or dream.

What's your dilemma? Have you been laid off? Or maybe you hate your job? You might have recently left the military service. Maybe you are a young single mother with kids to

Chapter One

take care of. Whatever the case, don't despair. If you are willing to try something new and do whatever it takes to succeed, then you are off to a good beginning. In this book, I will help you come to terms with your situation, guide you to the right attitude, and help you to start over or start a new business. I will share some basic rules to guide you. So make the commitment, and let's enjoy the journey.

Points to Review:

1. **Do you remember a time or event that changed or defined you?**

2. **What type of person do you want to become?**

3. **Are you where you want to be?**

    ➢ Personally

    ➢ Spiritually

    ➢ Financially

    ➢ Professionally

CHAPTER 2

Overcoming fears, making choices and goals, continuing to establish credibility

From Trenches to Triumph...

We are all faced with choices. You can choose to win or lose. You make choices each day. You make a choice to get up in the morning or stay in bed. Some choices become automatic while other choices require consideration. For instance, upon waking, we automatically get out of bed, but we choose to brush our teeth. What I want to do is to help you make productive choices that will lead to the success of your dream.

To be successful at anything, you need a positive, strong attitude. The first thing to know is that success is the result of many failures. What we do with those failures will determine our level of success. I have always believed that whatever the mind can conceive, the body can achieve. Several motivational speakers teach this idea. You will discover that you can achieve what you conceive if you believe. I want to fly, and although my body is not built for flying, I still find a way to fly. We need to make goals based on what we are passionate about. I know we are often told that we can do anything we set our minds to. And we can. Just be passionate about your goals and develop the right attitude for success.

So where do you start? One of your first projects should involve developing the right mindset. There are so many avenues available to you. Start with the bookstore. I have found many helpful books on self-improvement. We must

Chapter Two

be brutally honest with ourselves. We have to approach this new endeavor fully committed. Ask yourself this question: Am I willing to pay the price to reach my goals?

What is the price? For each of us this is different. You might have to be away from your family more than you want. You may have to attend school or special training courses. You may need to spend long hours at work. Or the price may not be any of these things. But it will take commitment and fortitude. If you are unwilling to make a commitment, then you are doomed to fail.

I copied this article from a book, and it helped me keep the right perspective. I still read it today when I am feeling down. I do not know who the author is, but I like the lessons conveyed. You should make a copy of this and read it often.

THE BOTTOM LINE

By Keith Kennedy

FACE IT...

NOBODY OWES YOU A LIVING!

What you achieve or fail to achieve in your lifetime is directly related to what you do, or fail to do.

From Trenches to Triumph…

No one chooses his parents or childhood
but you can choose your own direction.
Everyone has problems and obstacles to overcome
but that too is relative to each individual.

NOTHING IS CARVED IN STONE!

You can change anything in your life
if you want to badly enough.

EXCUSES ARE FOR LOSERS!

Those who take responsibility for their actions
are the real winners in life.
Winners meet life's challenges head on
knowing there are no guarantees
and give it all they've got.

It's never too late or too early to begin.
Time plays no favorites,
and will pass whether you act or not.

Chapter Two

> **TAKE CONTROL OF YOUR LIFE!**
>
> Dare to dream...take risks.
>
> If you aren't willing to work for your goals, don't expect others to.
>
> **BELIEVE IN YOURSELF!**

I think that most young people have been taught that we should look to others—government, companies, or families—to take care of us. Look around, how many thirty- to forty-year-olds are living with their parents? Don't get me wrong. Help should be available to people who really need it. The problem is that entitlement is an easy frame of mind to fall into. Think about what success entails. Successful people do what unsuccessful people don't do: work hard and persevere. So are you willing to put forth the effort?

When I had to accept the teacher's view that I was a slow reader, I made a decision. I would not stay in that group. I would improve. I decided not to accept the choice she made for me although doing so would have been easy since very little would have been expected of me. When you expect less, you get less. When you expect more, you get more. I did not realize the impact of my decision at the time, but it developed the core attitudes I have today. We must make our own decision. Otherwise, we let others determine our course in life.

You are the person you are today because of the choices you made or the choices others made for you. Now that is not all bad. Parents have to guide us and make some choices for us, such as the school we attend and possibly our religious background, which affects out morals and standards. Most of us had parents who did their best to help us be a productive member of society. Some of us had parents who didn't care or failed to instill values in us. That doesn't matter. We are still faced with a choice. Do we let others determine our success?

Somehow, I realized early in life that if I do things differently, I'll get a different result. I remember my aunts and how they viewed life. I can still hear them saying to me, "Dave, we may be poor, but we are proud, decent, and honest people." I didn't realize it then, but the underlying meaning was to accept that we were poor. Even at the age of twelve, I knew that this idea was not acceptable and thought to myself "to hell with this." I wasn't going to let anybody put thoughts in my head that I didn't agree with.

---

[1] Keith Kennedy. "The Bottom Line." *http://www.theabundanceproject.com/2014/09/face-it-nobody-owes-you-a-living/* January 4, 2017.

Chapter Two

The saying "Don't let others rent space in your mind" was real to me, and I was not going to accept my aunts' attitude. This decision helped me become who I am today. I would not accept an average life. You can rise above average. Make decisions that expand your horizons, decisions that you are passionate about. Start educating yourself on what you are passionate about.

One of the best educations is working for a sales organization where you will learn the core values of sales. Even if your ultimate goal isn't to sell products, you still have to sell yourself or sell your company's service. People buy a service or a product after they have bought you. Sales is an art. You don't have to be born a salesman. Learning salesmanship is hard work, and it can be applied to almost any situation. Knowing how to exchange thoughts and ideas that convey your conviction goes a long way in any company. There is always something new in sales training and techniques. Check out bookstores and the Internet for sales training materials. Earl Nightingale has a variety of good materials online.

Also, attend seminars, workshops, and training classes for your chosen field. Seminars can be costly, but they're well worth the expense. The training you receive is what I call "OJT" or" on-the-job training." It's practical because it can be implemented immediately in your field of choice.

From Trenches to Triumph...

When I first started in sales, I didn't realize that there were seminars available to salespeople. So I did a lot of reading instead. But there is a difference between reading books and attending live seminars. Sometimes the live seminars motivate you better than a book does because you tend to take action faster. I became a salesman in 1983 when there were very few training programs or seminars to attend. Today, searching the Internet and browsing through the large selections at bookstores you can easily find the resources and information to guide you in the right direction. Become a person who implements what you learned. Immediately implement what you have learned. Take action. That is the difference between successful people and unsuccessful people.

Remember that success means doing whatever it takes to accomplish our goals. Don't quit! Put forth the effort even when it's difficult to do so. Remembering on my third grade reading experience I realize now, that this was my defining moment in my life. I made up my mind that I was not going to be in that group. I could've accepted the choice made by my teacher. I knew I was better than that. We have to make a decision for ourselves or we are going to let others determine our destiny or course of life. Look at yourself. You are the person you are today because of the choices either you made or the choices others made for you. So right now, take the time to organize your choices, the things that you

Chapter Two

want to do, and the things that you want to change about yourself. Think about your current situation and determine to change it. It is up to you to become the person you want to be.

The next step is to set your goals and create a plan to reach them. Be willing to go beyond your goals. Many people have reached their goals and stopped setting new ones. Then they stopped improving. They become complacent and questioned if their hard work was worth it or not. If you're not learning, improving, and achieving something you wanted, you can become mentally stagnant. If you become complacent, you might lose.

Decide what you want to tackle. Over the years, I have had good mentors in the sales field, the best of these being a man called J.R. Cater. He enlightened me about the art of direct sales by working with me and leading by example. J.R. always set goals and worked to reach them. How did we set our goals in the field of sales? The same way you would with any other situation. We wrote our goals down. There is something about writing it down; it becomes real to you. Your mind immediately starts to map out a plan to accomplish your goals. So write down your goals and place them somewhere that you will see them every day.

From Trenches to Triumph...

Believe it or not, I always stick my written goals to my bathroom mirror. When I get up every morning and brush my teeth, guess what I read? Yep, my goals. This action will help kick start your brain into action. I also suggest that you say your plan out loud to yourself. "Today, I need to...," and then lay out a plan of action. You must plan your work before you execute your plan. Now, let's learn how to make that plan.

Points to Review:

1. **Can you identify what your fears are?**

2. **What choices have you made (good or bad)?**

    - **Personally**
    - **Spiritually**
    - **Financially**
    - **Professionally**

Chapter Two

3. Have you written down the goals for your?

> Month

> Year

> Decade

> Lifetime

CHAPTER 3

Vision comes before the plan

From Trenches to Triumph…

Once you have a clear vision in place, you will to need to shift your mindset. If this is the first time you have worked toward your vision or started your own business, you must realize that you are the boss now, the owner. You make all the decisions whether or not they are good or bad.

When you own your own business, you have to wear many hats: CEO, sales manager, customer service provider, delivery man/woman, and the list goes on. This means that you have to make decisions from a different perspective. The success of your company depends on you. Being the boss or CEO is not always a bed of roses. Take the time to realize that you are the one who will make the company a success or a failure. There are many rewards to owning your own business, but it's important to understand that there will be challenges. Since I was twenty-five, I have been my own boss for almost forty years. And believe me, I would not have it any other way. I have had good times and bad times, and have made good decisions and bad decisions. I love what I do, and I love owning my company.

FEAR

Everybody has fear. I am no different. You have to put fear in its proper place. Believe it or not, fear can keep you honest. One of my greatest fears is not being able to pay the company bills. I know each month I have to pay my suppliers or company overhead. If I don't follow through, I can lose my business. So I use that fear to motivate myself when I don't really feel like working. Sometimes, I am too sick or too tired, but I still go and do my job. One winter, I caught a cold that I couldn't get rid of. This continued for weeks. I was missing too many days at work, which meant that I was losing a lot of income. I needed to make some money. One night, I had a sales appointment, and I was as sick as a dog. For two and a half hours I gave my presentation. I cooked for eight people, did all the cleaning and kept a smile on my face. There were times I even leaned on the counter or held onto the sink to keep from falling over. Somehow, I made it. The need to pay my bills is what kept me going. Using that fear was a productive way to get me out of bed. Whatever fear you have, make it work for you. As a matter of fact, I earned enough that night to pay my mortgage and a few other bills. If I was working for someone else, I may have called in sick, wouldn't you? This is the difference between a passion and a job.

PERSONAL RISK

Sometimes you will have to take risks. When I moved back to Florida as an adult, I hoped to build a successful automobile

From Trenches to Triumph...

striping business. I was in my twenties and full of energy, big hopes, and a dream! I borrowed money from my wife's grandfather. With the help of my brother, I tried working with the local car dealer in the Orlando, Florida, area. If a stripe came off or the customer was in a wreck and needed repairs, the dealer needed to find the same company to match the striping. The problem with Florida was that a lot of striping companies were leaving town about as fast as they were coming in. Therefore, the dealers were very careful in whom they used. Since I was new in town, it was difficult to convince them that I would be reliable. My funds were disappearing fast. I had to do something because I didn't have enough money to last much longer. Once again, I was down to my last hundred dollars. I had a wife and son to provide for and a lot of bills. I was at my wits end. I had to make a decision. Do I take what I had left and continue to drive around to dealerships looking for work? Or do I just give up?

I still didn't want to work for anybody else. This was not an option for me. Don't get me wrong; if it came to the point of my family going without, I would certainly get a job. But I wanted to keep my full attention focused on my car striping business. My wife and I talked about a solution that would keep our vision alive. I called my mother in North Carolina, and she suggested that we see if there was a better reception from the car dealerships in her area. I had a little F-10 Datsun

Chapter Three

car that got over forty miles to the gallon. Gas at the time was only a dollar per gallon. For less than twenty dollars, I could drive to North Carolina and scout out the area. We prayed for the right direction. We left that Sunday morning and headed to North Carolina. I had to either succeed or go out of business. I did not want to lose my dream or my vision. We will revisit this story later.

FAMILY AND FRIENDS

One of the hardest obstacles to deal with is the feedback from friends and family. Believe it or not, the most destructive voices often come from those closest to us. It's not that they don't want the best for you, but it may be hard for them to understand your vision or your new profession. Many times, they may be projecting their own fear onto you or be reliving their past failures. I have watched many promising, young entrepreneurs be destroyed by the questions of their concerned parents. Here are some possible examples that some may ask you:

1. How much money will you make?

2. You know that most companies fail in the first year!

3. You have never run a company before.

4. You don't know what you are doing.

5. I know too many people who have tried that and failed.

6. Who do you think you are?

7. You never finish anything.

8. You don't know enough about running a business

You may have heard all of these before. I sure did. The night before I left to start a striping business in Colorado, a good friend of mine came by my house and begged me not to leave. He was so concerned that I would not succeed. He didn't want to see me fail. He offered to help with everything if I stayed home. I knew he was only worried about my family, but I also knew that I could make it. I had confidence in my own abilities. He didn't understand my vision. I wanted my own business. Needless to say, I did not listen to my friend and became very successful in Colorado. If I had listened to my friend and taken his advice, I would have given up on my vision. I may have earned a living working for him, but I wouldn't have been happy.

Many people don't want you to succeed because they are too afraid to try themselves. Don't get angry with them or resent

Chapter Three

them. That fear is their problem, not yours. I always think about what a top salesman once said, "Never take advice from someone who has never run a successful business for themselves before." They don't have the experience to be the expert. I suggest you talk to people who have done it before and been successful. Ask for their advice. Listen to what they have to say. Now, let's talk about the rewards.

UNLIMITED INCOME

One benefit of working for you versus working for someone else is the income. There is usually a limitation on the amount you can earn from a company. Working for you is a different story. You get to decide what your income potential will be. Let me give you an example of how you can set your own income level and figure out the work needed. Let's say you are interested in real estate. First, write down what you want to earn.

1. Annual income $100,000

2. Profession or Business   Realtor

3. Commission earned   3%

4. Average price of homes sold $180,000.

From Trenches to Triumph...

Now you have a plan. Let's figure out profit on two houses.

2 houses $360,000.   X   3%
            = $10,800.

1 house $180,000.   X   3%
            = $ 5,400.

5. Average houses sold monthly   2 to 3

If you notice, the income on two houses is over a hundred thousand dollars. But you will have overhead such as advertising, office supplies, gas costs. Also, you will have the referral fees. In other words, there's a cost to doing business.

Now is the time for a little more research. By studying the habits of a realtor who sells two or three houses a month, you can discover and follow the steps that will lead to your desired income. Is this easy? It depends on your attitude. I love my job, so I think it is easy. If you love what you are doing, you can be successful.

It all depends on how hard or how smart you work at selling. I know of realtors who sell four or more houses a month. One of them spends eighty thousand dollars a year on advertising and is one of the top realtors for her company. She accomplishes her goals and so can you.

Chapter Three

FREEDOM

The thing I cherish the most is the freedom I have in owning a business. I still work hard, but I set my own hours, and I love it. When I first started working I worked more hours than I wanted to, but I knew it would pay off in the long run. I now work about half the hours I used to and make the same money. I always look for ways to be more efficient. You may even hire people to do it for you and not have to do it all yourself. (Five people can do more than one person if they are trained properly.) Maybe traveling is your passion. Check out the travel industry, or look for a company that gives you the opportunity for a lot of traveling. This way you can make your job your passion. I heard of a couple who worked on a cruise ship for five years. They love traveling and meeting interesting people. It is up to you.

PASSION

I always knew I wanted to run my own business. My path started with roofing. I had some control of my income because my paycheck was based on production, but I was still working for someone else. When the construction business hit a recession, I started a new profession in the car striping business. Finally, I was my own boss, and I loved it! I could be creative, get paid for it, and could set my own income goals. When I first wanted to start my own business, I never thought it would be a car striping business. The automobile striping business was profitable, and I really enjoyed the creativity of auto graphics. As I became familiar with the business, I learned that a dealer might find ways to pay less for high quality work. So I always kept an eye out for something else that I could become involved in. This would come sooner than I had ever thought.

I was in a car wreck in the early eighties. My business was doing well, but because of the wreck, I was unable to bend and kneel to do the striping. I tried to pursue my business, but it became obvious that I could not maintain the pace. Manual labor is for the healthy and young. Again, I saw the need to change my profession. I reasoned that I would need a less physical job in which I could use my intellect above my brawn. This is how I found the wonderful world of sales. It became my new profession and has been all the way up to today. Your first business may be only a stepping stone to your vision or goal, so enjoy the journey. I have. Everything you experience in each endeavor will help you in your next one.

Sometimes change is uncomfortable but necessary. When I left Florida to check out North Carolina, I was fully convinced that I would be a success no matter where I relocated. After all, I had a family depending on me. We arrived in

Chapter Three

Reidsville, NC, late in the evening, and I started bright and early the next morning. I went straight to Danville, Virginia (a town only a few miles north of Reidsville). The first dealership I visited was a Pontiac dealership called Fuquay Pontiac. I walked into the showroom and saw only one person sitting in a chair. He was an older gentleman who was dressed in overalls. He asked if he could help me. I asked to see the sales manager. He said that the manager was in a meeting and wondered if he could help me. He was so nice and friendly that I introduced myself and told him what I did. He asked to see the pictures of my work. We spoke for about ten minutes, and I was glad to pass the time until I could see the manager. To my surprise, he introduced himself as Mr. Fuquay, the owner of the dealership. He said he would be glad to give me a chance to earn his business. I was floored. I told him I had to return to Florida for my truck and supplies. He said that when I returned he would have five cars ready that needed vinyl tops. I thanked him; we shook hands, and a deal was struck.

I was so excited that I wanted to line up another dealership, so I went to the Honda dealership. I showed Grover Adkins, the owner, pictures of my work and told him my plans to settle in the area. He said that he would give me all the work that I could handle. He did just that, and I worked at his dealership business until the day I sold my business years later. In fact, I worked for nearly all of my clients I sold out, except one. The dealers remained loyal to me, and I was loyal to them. I always went beyond what was expected in my service to them.

The first day, I talked to more dealers in the area and continued to set up more accounts. I felt good about each day's work and that I would have plenty of work once I had my truck and equipment with me. When I came back a few days later, Mr. Fuquay was true to his word. He had five vinyl tops ready for installation and had added some striping work. Mr. Atkins gave me all of his work and shut out anyone else he had previously used. I really enjoyed working with those small town dealerships. Each dealership treated me with respect, and they became friends as well as business associates.

Owning my own business had finally become a reality. I found that I used all of the skills I learned from my childhood. Remember my struggle to approach people on the streets when I sold peanuts? I had developed skills in my construction job and learned to think ahead to make the job faster as well as smoother.

So how can you get into action? I encourage you to follow these steps:

Chapter Three

1. Write down the skills you've developed through the years. You may even have your spouse or a family member help you.

2. Write down all your physical assets, such as money, tools, training, college degree, contacts, personal banker, friends who would invest time or money in your company. You will be surprised at what you might have.

3. List your job history. Rate how you liked or disliked each job. You never know what opportunity will come your way. I believe that when you give to others and help them have a better lifestyle through your business, it will come back to you in the future.

4. Think about what you really enjoy doing and develop a business strategy to match it. I might help spark some ideas, but remember it is up to you and what you like.

After you decide what you want to do, it's time to be really honest with yourself. This is when you list your strengths and, yes, your weaknesses. You must acknowledge what you are good at and what you need to improve. For instance, I hate using the telephone, but meeting people in person is one of my strong points. I still use the phone when I must, but I know that it's one of my weaknesses. I work better when I am in front of my client where I can see him or her eye to eye.

As an entrepreneur, you need to be willing to think about things differently than when you worked for someone else. The moment you go back to thinking like an employee and lose sight of your vision, you lose. You can definitely do it; just keep your vision of who you want to be and where you want to go in front of you at all times. Once, we interviewed a young man named Steve for a company position, and after we'd accepted him, I took about an hour to explain the troubles he might experience once he told people his chosen career. First, I asked him what his dream or vision was that he had for himself in five years. I could see his desire to become a professional who ran his own business. But it would take more than a desire. I explained to him that his family and friends might not understand his vision. Some might try to talk him out of his new endeavor. Some would try to protect him from his disappointments. Others would discourage him because they didn't want to see someone else succeed. It made me think of the old cliché: "misery loves company." I told him to look at the person who was trying to discourage him and see what he has to offer. If that person says, "You can't do that. I have heard too many people fail at that," what is his motive? Is it to help or stop him. I told him to be prepared to hear all the negative responses from close

Chapter Three

friends and family. I told him that the majority of people he meets will try to discourage him while a small handful of people will support his decision. Sure enough, the very next day he told me that only a few supported him. He still had the desire in his eyes, and I do believe that this young man will go far in his journey to success.

Each of us has an inner strength that we can tap into. You have to reach deep down and pull it out. For me, it is the burning desire to win. I hate to quit. I have always felt that once you quit on one thing, it becomes easier to quit again. I believe we are all winners. The truth of the matter is that you started out a winner by beating out millions of others to be conceived in the womb. You started out a winner, so why not continue? We have to test ourselves to know what type of person we are. So please, use your potential, and do not waste it on self-doubt.

Without a vision, purpose or goal, it is too easy to quit or give up. In the next chapter, I will talk to you about the kind of training that you will need. Are you ready?

From Trenches to Triumph...

Points to Review:

1. **What are you passionate about?**

2. **Is your vision equal to your passion?**

3. **Are you willing to take personal risks to achieve your vision?**

CHAPTER 4

Education can come from different venues

From Trenches to Triumph...

By now, you should have taken the time to really look inward and pull out your vision. There is a misconception about being your own boss. No one is born a leader. Skills must be developed through education and hard work. No matter what you pursue, you have to learn your craft. A number of ways to learn are available to you. I think "on-the-job training" is one of the best ways. For example, when I had become a roofer, I wanted to be not only fast, but also proficient at roofing. My boss explained that I needed to develop an orderly process. He suggested that I should lay the shingles so many feet apart so that I would not waste time bringing each bundle of shingles separately to the roof. Fewer steps meant less wear and tear on the body. Then he said to learn how to finger my nails ahead of time (a process of holding a bundle of nails that you can systematically slip through your fingers). He told me to practice fingering my nails while I was watching TV or driving to work. He said, "That way when we need you on the roof, you will already have developed a little speed." So I practiced just as he said, and it worked. I became fast and kept up with the other workers. They were great guys to work with, but they played practical jokes on me if I slowed down. Sometimes, they would nail my shoe to the roof. Needless to say, it didn't take long for me to pick up my speed. Because of my work ethic, I was rewarded with progressive raises in my paycheck.

Chapter Four

If you have an opportunity to attend a trade school, you can improve your skills. There are night classes at most colleges, and a number of courses are offered from business courses to blue collar jobs. Check out your local schools, and talk to the counselors. Many schools will give you an evaluation exam that can show where your strengths are. Just keep in mind that these institutions will train you to be part of a herd. By that I mean that they teach you to follow a certain program with no room for innovation or thinking outside the box. Now that does not mean to throw caution to the wind. Just keep your vision and goals in front of you and be open to new concepts or ideas.

Each time I had to change professions, there was a learning curve. When I was laid off at the Safeway bakery, I was only eighteen years old. It was 1967, and jobs were hard to find. The United States draft was in effect. I had a 1A status, so I could be called to duty on very short notice. Employers were skeptical about hiring people with 1A status for that very reason, but the bakery manager had given me a job anyway. Every day, the manager would walk through and talk to me while I was working. I was usually washing stacks of cookie trays. I worked fast so that I could finish my duties in an eight hour shift, so the manager would not have to pay me overtime. As he watched me, he could not believe how hard I worked. It became a habit; he would drop by and talk to me while I washed all the trays. Then one day, he told me that the bakery had to lay someone off and, unfortunately, it was me. He told me that I could finish out the week. I couldn't believe it. I had worked so hard and never missed a day nor was I ever late. I needed this job. I didn't know what I was going to do. The manager felt bad, and I knew he had a hard time laying me off. Then he said, "Dave, if I can get you on part-time as a bag boy until I can figure out how to help keep you here, will you take the job? Remember, it is only part-time." I was grateful and took the job. I figured that I could do this while I looked for another job. There I went, learning another job.

I had always thought of myself as a hard worker, but now I began to develop skills that were what you might call innovative. I noticed that the bag boys packed groceries slowly. Being full of energy, I decided to work at four checkout stands at once. I would put a started bag at each check stand and run back and forth putting items into each bag. This got me recognized for my industriousness. No one else could bag up to four checkout stands at once. The clerks noticed my ingenuity, and they would request me to bag their items. Another thing I noticed was that when a clerk called for customer's groceries to be carried out the bag boys walked slowly to the front of the stores. So as soon as I heard the service call I would run, not walk, to the front and take the grocery cart for the customer. Regular

Chapter Four

customers remembered me because I would joke around with them, making them laugh at silly things. It was a small town, and before long, the customers would ask for me to load their groceries into their car. When you have to change jobs, learn to look at the positive side of things. Look for ways to make the job fun and easy. No matter what the job is, there are things you can do to make it better, and you can learn by observing. If you can find ways to improve the process, you will get noticed for your ingenuity.

So I did my job with gusto. I would always challenge myself to be better at my job. I would create work for myself so that I would stand out from the others. In other words, self-educate or educate yourself. You have a mind, so use it. In the grocery store, most of the bag boys would ignore the service call to bring the carts back into the store. Not me. I would run outside and gather them up as fast as I could. Also, when I took customers groceries to their car, I would gather the shopping carts in the parking lot as I returned inside. After a while, I started to like my job. I didn't realize it at the time, but I was developing an entrepreneurial attitude. Being creative is a big part of the entrepreneur's spirit. No matter what road you chose, whether it be trade schools or on-the- job training, be creative and make it your own. Take advantage of every training opportunity available and check out books that can enhance your skills.

From Trenches to Triumph...

I am an entrepreneur first, businessman second, but my profession is direct sales. As an entrepreneur, you should learn the "art of sales." There is a big difference between being an order taker and knowing the "art of sales." The level of success you have will be directly dependent on your knowing the difference between these two.

Education is very important. When faced with a career change, you can either jump right in without a plan or chose to educate yourself and devise a plan to succeed. Most small businesses fail their first year. The same can be said about starting a new career. The key is proper education or experience. So how do you educate yourself? You should draw from past experiences, apply what you learned, and learn from the mistakes that you have made. Mistakes are only temporary setbacks; good skills and techniques can be learned through this experience. Evaluate some of the things you've done in the past. Maybe you worked with the Boy Scouts, volunteered as an intern in school, or helped your parents in their business. Remember the social contacts you've made from these experiences. They can be used in the future. Events and projects completed can be used as "letters of recommendation" to be referred back to in the future. These true life experiences are skills that you will carry with you for a lifetime. Look at your prior schooling and list your accomplishments. These can and will translate to further skills in the years ahead, just as

Chapter Four

selling peanuts on the streets of Gainesville, Florida, taught me how to approach people professionally. I had to change my way of selling or else I would be replaced by someone with greater skills. I found a way to succeed no matter how uncomfortable it was. Today, after thirty plus years in sales, nothing has changed. When my sales are low, I always try to further my education by reading any book on business or sales techniques that I can find. And when I do, I always find a new tip for success. I never use the word "impossible" I "break it apart to "I'm possible."" There is always a way to accomplish your goals.

Some of you might have the opportunity to attend certain schools, or you might have grown up in a family-owned business. Take advantage of whatever is available to you. I, on the other hand, had to learn each career by teaching myself. Self-education is useful and works to your advantage sometimes. You become focused on your current situation. For example, when I had to change professions from grocery clerk to construction, I received an offer to work for my wife's cousin in the roofing business. I jumped at the chance. I knew that my dream of being a business owner was never going to happen at Safeway. Since most of my family was in the construction industry, I was familiar with it. With hard work and dedication, I could become a roofing contractor. This change would bring me closer to my vision of becoming my own boss.

From Trenches to Triumph...

What is your vision or business goal? Today, there are so many choices. Is it owning your own company or maybe striving to be number one under someone else's business? I had a childhood dream of being a Navy pilot. When I sold peanuts, one of my regular stops was the Navy recruiting office. I could not wait until I got to the recruiting office every day. The guys there were great guys. They made a card that said I was an honorary member of the Navy. They shared their experiences, and I loved listening to them. They knew I wanted to be a Navy fighter pilot, so they went out of their way to make me feel special. They encouraged me, and because of them, I set my goal to become one of the Navy's finest pilots. Every night, I would dream of flying a jet. I kept that dream for a long time. When it came time for my dream to come true, the Vietnam Conflict was in full swing. On the day of my seventeenth birthday, I headed straight to the Navy recruiting station. I was so excited and ready to become what I had always dreamed about. Then the unexpected happened, and my lifelong dream was shattered. The Navy was not accepting recruits. Their quota was filled, and I was told that I would have to wait two to three more years. I was devastated. How could this happen? But it was no problem, I decided to join the Air Force instead. There was nothing wrong with enlisting in the Air Force although I was a little disappointed because it was my dream to be in the Navy. My father had been in the Navy, and I always admired him for his sacrifice and

Chapter Four

wanted to be a part of that too. Unfortunately, the Air Force was not accepting any more people either, so my dream would have to wait for a later time. Life does not always work out the way you want it to. So when something like this happens, you go on. Although my dream of flying and becoming a fighter pilot never came to fruition, I still love to see the pilots of the Naval Air Station fly daily over my home in Pensacola, Florida. I still dream that I am one of them. Gary Coxe, a good friend of mine who is a pilot, let me fly his plane and gave me some flying lessons. I loved it. I met Gary at one of his seminars in the early 90's, and we became good friends. He told me that if I was ever in the area to stop by his office for a visit. A few weeks later, I was traveling from Daytona Beach to Tampa, and his office was just off the freeway close to Tampa. We visited a while, and he asked what some of my goals were. I mentioned that I always wanted to fly an airplane. I didn't realize that he owned a plane and that the airport was only a few blocks away. He said, "How would you like to reach one of your goals today?" The next thing I knew, we were at the airport, and I was in the pilot's seat. He told me what to do, and I did just so. I couldn't believe we were in the air, and I was flying a plane. What a thrill! Over the years, I have flown with him, and he always lets me take the controls and fly. Years later, he opened a helicopter school, and the next time I visited, guess what? I flew his helicopter. That was a little bit scary for me, but Gary was right there to talk me

From Trenches to Triumph...

through it. This just goes to show you that your dreams may not come true when you want them too, but that doesn't mean that they will never happen. In the next chapter, you can start implementing your plan.

Points to Review:

1. **Are you an order-taker or an innovator?**

2. **What is the difference between an order-taker and business person?**

3. **Never stop learning.**

CHAPTER 5

Know your craft

From Trenches to Triumph...

Now there are different ways to sell your product of service. What I'd like to do now is cover different types of sales techniques. They can be applied to any type of business and will help you sell your product or close the sale. Remember, a sale has to be made in order for a business to make money.

First, you need to know your product or service. Second, you have to learn closing techniques. Closing is asking the right questions to make the buyer want the product. The better you can close, the more sales you will make. You do not have to be a high-pressure salesman. That type of salesperson has too many cancellations (buyer's remorse) and has a hard time getting referrals for their customers. I prefer soft-sell techniques. I let my customers decide to buy with my help. People like buying things, but they don't want to be sold anything. So the less you sound like a salesman, the better. I have always told my salespeople that people will tell you what they want and when they want it and how they will pay for it-- if you ask the right questions.

Here are nine closing techniques to guide you. Practice them as much as possible. Make them second nature. Don't have a monotone or robotic sounding presentation. You have to sound like you care and are trying to help clients make an informed decision. So let's begin.

Chapter Five

1. There are liars and buyers.

2. The first NO means nothing.

3. Birds of a feather flock together.

4. People like to own, not buy.

5. Never judge a book by its cover.

6. Ask for the order.

7. You get what you pay for.

8. An open door is an open mind.

9. Plan your work, work your plan.

1. **There are two types of prospects, liars and buyers.** The first thing you need to learn is that people lie. That's right, they'll lie to you. It's their defense mechanism. Here are a few.

    ➢ "I can't afford it."

> "I don't make decisions on the spur of a moment."

> "I always talk over major purchases with my parents."

> "I have to pray about it."

> "I'm just gathering information at this time."

In most cases, that's just a defense. I want you to ignore these responses the first time they are presented. This is not their final answer to the sale. What they're really telling you is that you have not given them enough information for them to make an informed decision. There is also the Feel, Felt, and Found method. It is used by a lot of sales professionals. Here's an example: "I understand how you feel. I felt the same way, but what I've found out is that our clients saw savings in only a short time." Or you could use this one: "But what we've found is that our customers are happier not having to repair the product all the time." Find out why your customers love your product or service and use that in your closing.

2. **Ignore the first NO.** Take each objection one at a time and restate it back to your prospect verbally. If they made the statement "I can't afford it,"

Chapter Five

look them in the eye and repeat it back to them. "You can't afford it. Let me ask you a question. Is it the price or the cost you can't afford?" Let them defend their statement. If they say it is the price, then breakdown the price. For example, if they are interested in painting the outside of their house. The premium brand may cost twice as much as the cheaper one. So you have to make a comparison. You might say, "I know this brand will cost more, but let me explain the difference. The cheaper brand lasts only four years before you have to paint the house again whereas the premium brand lasts for fifteen years. So in the long run, it will save you from having to repaint your house at least twice. So which one will be better for you, paint your house three times for the lower price or once at the higher price?" Rationally provide the information to rebuff the objections. When the objections have been covered, summarize the advantages and ask for the purchase. By a process of elimination, stop them in their tracks, so to speak, and redirect them to the reasonableness of obtaining the product or service being offered. In most cases, it may require you to use several types of closing techniques before an actual sale is made. Remember, everyone is taught by parents, peers, and teachers not to sign anything.

3. **Birds of a feather flock together.** If your company requires you to obtain referrals, be wise when doing so. In my cookware business, people associate with people who think the same way and make some of the same purchases. It seems pretty consistent that people who have money associate with other people who have money. The same applies to people with bad credit. Why? Because bad credit is no big deal them. If your prospect has good credit, no doubt, his friends will too. This is not a hard fast rule, but it is most often true. You can use the credit rating of the current prospect to gauge the referrals and how much time you give in pursuing appointments with them.

4. **People like to own not buy.** People like to own nice things, and they pride themselves on making good decisions when purchasing them. It has to be their idea, and then they are comfortable with their decisions. If they feel you sold them something that they really didn't want or need, cancellations are more likely to occur, and you might become known as a high-pressure salesperson. So learn to ask questions and find out what they like. People know what they want, not what they need. In the cookware business, I used to ask, "Are you health conscious or not?" This question helped me talk

Chapter Five

more on health or convenience. Know the features and benefits of your service or product.

5. **Never judge a book by its cover.** When I was in the automobile striping business, a salesman told me a real life experience that he had. He was working at a Lincoln Dealership, and a man wearing old work clothes drove on the lot and began looking at a Lincoln. Of course, the salesman deduced the man could never afford to purchase a new car. The salesman was in no hurry to assist him and instead watched the man look around the lot several times in anticipation of assistance. When none came, the man drove off the lot. The salesman didn't think again about the man who, in his mind, would have just wasted his time until he saw the man return about an hour later come back to the lot. He came into the showroom and requested to speak to the manager. The salesman promptly got the sales manager and overheard a very troubling conversation. You see, the unkempt man had been doing some yard work for his wife and gotten an idea to surprise his wife with a new car. Then man didn't want to change his clothes, so he jumped into the car and came to the lot. Upon not receiving assistance to see a car, he had left and went to the Cadillac dealer just up the road. He had bought two

From Trenches to Triumph…

cars. The man thought "If the Lincoln dealership didn't assist me because of my appearance, maybe I'd better let them know that appearances can be deceiving." Don't let this happen to you in your business. Another similar experience happened to my mentor J.R. when he was twenty-one. He was selling cookware and had a large organization making many sales. He drove by a dealership and saw a red Buick Wildcat. He stopped and wanted to take it for a test drive. The salesman chuckled when J. R. asked for the keys to test drive the car. The salesman hesitated and asked. "Are you going to finance it?" thinking he would get rid of him since there was no way he would be able to finance the car since he was so young. J.R asked, "Well, how much is it?" The salesman quoted the price. J.R. said, "I'll just pay cash" and pulled the money out of his pocket. Being inexperienced he paid full price for the car. Don't let this happen to you in your business.

6. **Ask for it.** Nothing can be attained unless you ask! Salesmen lose every day for the simple reason that they don't ask for the sale. A few years back, I trained a new recruit who did a very good demonstration, but she had a condescending attitude. She was so high-minded that she never heard a prospect

Chapter Five

ask a closing question. Right then she should have answered by asking, "If the product could do that for you, does that sound like something you'd be interested in seeing?" She would have secured the first sales and had the opportunity to go on to secure more sales if other prospects were attending. Instead, she continued through her program. I got up from my chair, and asked, "Which set do you think would fit your needs?" The customer answered, and I wrote up the sale. I let her finish her dinner, and when we got in the car, I asked her how she thought she did. We had an older couple and a younger couple on the dinner show. She thought the older couple would've bought, but it was the younger couple that I was able to sell to. I asked her why she didn't consider the younger couple, and she said that it was because of their age. She had predetermined her prospect based on her assumptions not on the prospects' responses and questions throughout the dinner. I told her she was losing sales because she was not actually asking her prospects' to buy. I told her that the young couple wanted the product and that she had ignored them completely. When I pulled the paperwork from my bag, she was astounded. She had no idea that I had secured the sale. I gave her credit for the order and sternly charged her to "listen to your prospects!"

She took the advice to heart; now in her seventies, she is still in the cookware business and is a top producer.

I went to a sales convention with my company, and one of the speakers impressed me so much. I was new in direct sales. When he got on stage, he asked if anyone had five hundred dollars. Quite a few held up their hands. The speaker picked an audience member, and the speaker gave the audience member five hundred dollar bills. Then the speaker asked if anyone had a diamond cross pen. Quite a few hands went up, and the speaker got one. Then he asked for a beautiful lady to come up. Then the speaker said, "I have only been up here two minutes and look what I have, five hundred dollars, a diamond cross pen, and a beautiful lady. How did I get this? The speaker said I ask for it." I got the point. Funny thing is that is the only thing I remember. But it helped me so much in my career. Don't be afraid to ask for the order. People would ask me how I got so many cash orders instead of finance orders. I would simply say that I asked for it.

7. **You get what you pay for.** I knew when I started in sales that I wanted to sell only quality products. I knew from experience that if you buy cheap you get cheap. You get what you pay for. On one of my first jobs in construction, I bought a cheap tape

Chapter Five

measurer. I was told to buy a Stanley tape measure, but it cost three times more than the cheaper one. In one hour, the tape measure broke, and I was off to buy the one recommended. I lost work time which cost me more in the long run. Lesson learned! If you sell a quality product, then you can use the quality of your product as part of your sales pitch.

8. **Open door/open mind.** If you have a product that you sell from door to door, always remember that people who have their front doors open and just have the screen door open are friendly people. They tend to listen when someone comes to their door. So my policy has always been Open Door, Open Mind.

9. **Plan your work and work your plan.** You must know what you want to accomplish in your business and how to accomplish it. I suggest that you write it down. It will become more real to you this way. A sale is made in every presentation. Either you sell clients your product, or they sell you. In other words they do not buy what you are selling. They sold you by not buying. So if you are a true professional, take charge, and get the sale. There is a difference between what we in the field call hard sales and

soft sales. Those who use the hard sale approach are usually car salesmen, timeshares, home repair folks, and vacuum salesman. It is an effective way to sell, but I prefer a soft sale approach. This includes using a variety of closing tools. These are tried and proven to be effective. What you have to do is find out what your company uses that is successful. Talk to the top salesmen. I learned a lot by asking questions and working with the top producers. Most of them are glad to help you only if you ask.

Points to Review:

1. **Can you tell the difference between a liar and a buyer?**

2. **People want to be owners.**

3. **Develop your business plan, and then work it!**

CHAPTER 6

Implementing Your Plan

From Trenches to Triumph...

We have covered making your plan, your education, and now, it's time to implement your plan. I have always followed my plans with action. I believe in "do it now." Before deciding on my plan, I research. You don't want to go off half-cocked. This can be time-consuming and costly. All your planning is futile if you do not take action.

Set your starting date. Write it down. Follow up with what your actions will be to work after the staring date. Picture your business in your mind. See it being successful and your taking action. Make it real to yourself. Start acting as if it is a reality. Get into the mode. Become your business.

Let's say you want to open your business by January 1st You may need a few months in order to have everything in place. So start your research in the fall of the year prior. If your business is sales and you are going to be the distributor of a certain product, I strongly recommend that you visit your supplier to meet the people you will be dealing with. Don't just be someone on the phone who calls and orders. People like to know who they are working with. Sometimes, I can't meet them first, so I spend time on the phone talking to the person whom I will be working with and start bonding. I want them to enjoy our conversations and like me. If you have a good relationship with your supplier, you'll have

Chapter Six

better results when a problem arises. And believe me, this will happen. I deal with my supplier mainly on the phone. Always be friendly, and I always ask them how they are doing. When I talk to my supplies who live up north in the winter, I always joke about the weather with them because it is usually nice weather where I live. They love that I do this.

You will need to have a business address to put on all of your business papers. If you are going to work out of your home, use that address and also have a P.O. Box number. I have all my mail go to the P.O. Box number because it is safer. I use a UPS store because it receives all of my packages. If you have merchandise and work out of your home, you might not always be home. You wouldn't want your boxes sitting outside because they can get stolen or they could be subject to the weather. If you are going to have an office, the UPS delivers during business hours. I always had my office in a complex with other offices so that if I was not there UPS would deliver it to one of the other offices. You will need to know your neighbors. You will probably have to receive some of their packages as well. I strongly recommend that you have an office if you plan to hire people. It tends to stay on a business level. You want to be a business and not friends, so to speak. Remember you are running a business not a social club. If you do hire friends they may think they have special privileges, expect to be paid more than others and you will make exceptions when they don't follow company rules. You can be friendly, but try to keep it professional.

Next, set up your business as a sole-proprietor, LLC, sub-chapter S, or C-corp. with your city and state sales tax division. Talk to a lawyer, preferably a tax or corporate one. Get your federal tax number, business licenses, and sales tax number. Your CPA can help you with the forms. Then, you can start your business account at your bank. Don't wait until the last minute to do this. You will save a lot of heartache and problems if you start your business account soon. I recommend setting up a merchant credit card account with your bank. Or, if you are on the Internet you can use something like PayPal or the Square. Nothing is worse than not being able to process an order because clients can't pay you.

If you are selling a product that requires a bank or institutional finances, I recommend that you establish the proper connections with your finance companies and have your paperwork in order. I have more than one finance company. I have one that does mainly A credit paper, and then I have one that takes B and C paper. So if you have only A paper credit, you will lose some of your credit orders. The difference between the A and B is the credit score. A paper usually pays from 90 percent to a 100 percent of the

Chapter Six

amount of sale. B and C paper pays from about 50 percent to 80 percent. I look at it this way. 70 percent of something is better than 100 percent of nothing. Also, if you have sales people, you can deliver a product, and they make some money instead of nothing. I usually pay 20 percent commission for sales if the sale is an A paper finance. If the sale is a B or less, I pay half of the 20 percent commission. It keeps the morale up if your employees can make something on the sale. It is up to you. Take care of your salespeople. They have to make a living as well. If a person is working for you and makes a sale, his wife or husband usually wants to know if they made any money. As long they are bringing home a paycheck, their mate is more willing to support a 100 percent commission job. Think strongly about this. This applies mainly to direct sales. Department stores will handle it in their own way. Usually, they require a higher credit score. Even some companies do their own financing in house, and then they are able to make the profit on the interest. Watch out for the fees. Some companies charge you for everything.

I also recommend that you use non-recourse paper. Full recourse means you co-sign the note. I use only non-recourse paper. The finance company takes the risk, and you will not have chargeback. Lately, the finance companies require that the first payment be made to become non-recourse. I understand the reason for that. Some companies try to cheat the finance companies. They hurt the entire industry. What I do is take care of my finance companies because without them, I can't deliver a lot of my sales. If someone is slow to make a payment, then the finance company will call to let you know. I will either call or go to the customer and find out the problem. Most of the time, I can take care of it and keep both the customer and the finance company happy. It is your company, so take care of the problems ASAP.

Now that you have all of these things taken care of, it is time to hire your employees. This is where most businesses have problems. Whether you hire one person or ten people, you want to find the right people for the right job. In my business, we had a test called a personality profile that would determine the type of individual the applicants were. You will need to find a test that relates to your type of business that will help you. We knew from the start what we had to do to develop the sales person. The test was so accurate that we could determine if employees needed to be supervised or if they could work on their own without supervision. It also told us if they took orders well or if they could work well with people. This test was pretty accurate. The traits that were brought out by the test were not written in stone. If someone was weak in a certain area, we can help them overcome it. I know one of the problems that people

Chapter Six

face that showed up on the test was that they will work and learn very fast but will not stay in that job field. Once we knew that, we were able to know the challenges that they faced, so we worked on those to help them stay interested in the job. This way they could maintain a good working relationship within the company.

After hiring employees, you must set up an office. There are two things that you must have. The first thing is to have a company policy manual. This is helpful when you hire an employee because the employee will know what the company expects and what is required of them. In your company's policy manual, I also recommend that you have a company vision and a company statement. The second thing is a training manual. You want to be able to take a new person and within a limited amount of time be able to have that person trained and ready to start. If you do these two things first, I will guarantee you will have fewer problems later on.

When you hire new employees, I would recommend that you give them each a company manual and a training manual. Tell them to become very familiar with the company manual and the company policies. In most direct sales businesses, a flip chart is used in the presentation. And some companies use PowerPoint presentations. It doesn't matter which one you choose; both are effective.

In your training manual, you will want to design your training manual in sections. I recommend that you use three sections. The first section could be flip chart of direct sales or have a presentation. The second section should show your demonstration process. The third section should be your summary that you pitch to the client and close, in other words asking for the order. It all depends on your company and the products that are offered. I like using three sections. It also helps when you are training. I would always train in three sections. Once the person was proficient, by role playing, in one section, I would then move on to the next section. Also, when you are having sales training classes you work on one of these sections. I know that each profession has its own procedures, so find out the best way to teach.

The first section should be the introductory or warm up of your presentation. One of the things that I like to do is tell the client who I am, tell them the company that I work with, and tell the client what I am going to do. Then I ask a few questions in order to get a little feedback from the prospective clients. For instance, in my cookware business, I usually ask three questions. The first question is, "Who does the cooking?" The second question is, "Who does the grocery shopping?" And the third question is, "Are you health-conscious or would you like to be?" Depending on the answers that I receive back, I would adjust my power

Chapter Six

statements in my flip chart to these responses. For example if I heard someone say "I hate to cook," then during my flip chart I would ask questions such as, so you really hate to cook or is it that you do not have the time to cook?" Or I would ask, "Would you like to be able to cook and enjoy it?" Now, during my presentation, I am able to discern the prospect's needs. During my demonstration I would ask, "Isn't this easy? Can't you see yourself doing this? If you could prepare a meal like this that is hardly any work, don't you think you might like to cook a little more often?" So after your warm-up, you start your flip chart. The average attention span of most people is typically twenty minutes. You want to design your flip chart to last between fifteen to twenty minutes in length. Also in your flip chart, be sure to have colorful pictures and power statements. Having your power statements and your presentation in pictures and written form helps the prospects retain your information. Also using humor at key points helps your prospect to remember up to seven times as much. There was a study done at Harvard, I believe, on how important humor is in communicating. Also, humor relaxes your clients or prospects as well as your demonstration.

If you are demonstrating a product such as cookware, water filters, vacuum cleaners or cleaning supplies, you must involve your prospects. I do this with questions. For instance, if one of their answers to the questions was "I hate to cook," then you would use a tie-back statement like this: "Mary, you said you hated to cook right? Well, I just showed you how all you have to do is put the food in the pan and listen for the whistle right? Once you hear that, all you have to do is turn it down and forget it until you are ready to eat. In fact, you can leave it on the stove for five minutes or five hours, and your food will still be ready to serve. I do believe that you could do that, don't you? And remember eating at home saves you a lot of money, right?" I always try to ask questions that end in their answering, "Yes." The prospect's spouse might answer that they want to eat healthy. So ask the prospect this question, "I remember that you said that you wanted to eat healthier, right? Then I am sure you can see the value of eating at home. I was able to show you how to cook in half the time normally spent in the kitchen preparing a meal and I used no water and oil. So let me ask you, "Did you see the health benefits by using this method?" Now, let me ask you another question, "If you ate at home more often do you see the money you will save?" What you want to do is continue asking questions. Also, one thing that is very important: you need to listen to their answers and acknowledge their responses. If you are not listening to them, then they will stop answering your questions because they will feel like you aren't listening to them. Always be respectful. This has worked as my approach in my business, but it is the same approach although you will tailor it to your business pitch.

Chapter Six

Role playing your flip chart or presentation with other colleagues will help you become a better demonstrator. It is better to learn in the office so that you will make fewer mistakes on your presentation. I knew when I trained my sales people that they would say they knew the presentation well. As soon as I would have them present the flip chart for me, they would realize that they needed to practice more. I taught page by page until they knew the presentation. I would have them do the first page and then the second page. I know that repeating the chart over and over helps them to become proficient. So as they would learn each page, I would have them go back to the first page and repeat it up to the page they just memorized. Once they understood the process and how to present the information, I would tell them to go home and practice in front of their mirror and put it in their own words as long as it matched the verbiage on the flip chart. Once they mastered that, I would let them do that on their presentation. I would watch and write down notes that I could share with them after the dinner show.

It all depends on the presentation. In the cookware presentation, there were four parts to the program. First, the flip chart. Second, the cooking demo. Third was the soda test which is comparing the cookware to other brands of cookware. Fourth, was the close. They were all important, and each had a purpose.

Some presentations have only a flip chart, or what we call a canned presentation. A canned presentation was simple. You say the same thing on every appointment. And yes, it can become boring. It is up to the presenter to make it lively. The better you present the presentation, the bigger the reward.

Every company has a way of presenting its product. It is up to you to learn how the company wants the product presented. I have been in direct sales for so long that it is hard to relate to the way a regular business operates on an hourly or a set monthly income salary job. But I must say, the training you receive in direct sales usually will apply in all aspects of your life.

Let's review the concepts I have discussed in the chapter.

1. Keep your vision alive.

2. Write it down.

3. See it.

4. Make a training manual for your company.

5. Have a good training program.

Chapter Six

Points to Review:

1. **Do it now!**

2. **What are the administrative rules that govern your business model?**

3. **Hiring the wrong people can devastate your business.**

CHAPTER 7

Dealing with Failure

From Trenches to Triumph...

When my publisher recommended a chapter on failure, I had to step back and reflect on why he wanted this. I hate failures and do not like to think about them. Then it dawned on me that without failures we would not learn. Sometimes failures are answers to another problem. A lot of products that we use today are accidents or failures. I will not go into what they are right now, but I do want you to look at mistakes or failures as part of the process to success.

My son started to help me with this book because he was there when most of my businesses began. I have heard how he perceived what I accomplished from his childhood to today. Some of the things I thought were not so effective or successful had a positive effect on my son. For instance, I thought I worked too much when I first started my automobile striping business and felt guilty about the time I spent working late so many nights. Then when my son decided to help organize my book and help with some of the stories, I was shocked by his perception of events. Here is one that pulled on my heartstrings. This happened while we were driving to Orange Beach, Alabama, one day. We were discussing my book, and I mentioned what I felt were some of my failures. He looked at me and said, "Dad, you did what you had to do to provide for the family. I remember you working late some nights, and you would have mom take me to where you were working. By my being there with you,

Chapter Seven

I learned some valuable lessons I still use today. You would stop and eat dinner with us, and then you would run around and play with me. You taught me the value of work. You taught me the value of family. You taught me the value of how a family deals with what they have. I know that chasing me around the cars at the dealership late at night while I was on my hot wheels seems like a small thing, but they are some of my fondest memories as a child." As I heard my son remind me of some of the things we have gone through and how we dealt with them, I became very proud of my son. He has had his ups and downs like every other child, but what I realized at that moment was that what I thought might have been failures or weaknesses were just stepping stones in life. This is how we learn to deal with situations we each face.

Now, when I look at my son, he is not just a little boy, but a grown man with values I instilled in him: family, hard work, going the extra mile for your work, and most importantly the love of your family. No matter what happens, if a family has love, you can overcome most challenges.

So I learned a valuable lesson myself just by looking back at what I thought were failures. Never forget your family and the support you have from them. Put your family ahead of your business. Businesses come and go, but family can and should always be there.

From Trenches to Triumph...

I am the type of person who does not like to talk about failures. That is why this chapter will be short and to the point. You need failures in order to succeed. This is how we learn. If everything was easy, then nothing would stand out or be different. There is a saying: "Failure is not an option," and I look at things that way. But there is more to it. Without failures there would be no options to choose from. Every failure can have a good outcome if you look at it as a stepping stone in reaching an objective.

Think of the steps to put failures in perspective.

1. Evaluate.

2. Accept responsibility for your actions.

3. Seek advice.

4. Research new solutions.

5. Take action now.

6. Be thankful for what you have.

7. Have the right attitude.

Chapter Seven

8. Give back.

1. Evaluate:

When you have a failure, the first thing you need to do is step back and take a good long, hard look at what has just happened or occurred. Sometimes it is not as bad as you think it is. Time helps as well as a new set of eyes. Talk to someone who has been through a problem like yours. I have a lot of people I stay in contact with who are my friends as well as mentors. Don't be ashamed or afraid of telling someone what has just happened. You will be surprised at the advice or help you might receive. Always remember who helped you, and when the time presents itself, you maybe return the favor. Like Zig Ziglar used to say, "Help enough people get what they want and you will get what you want." I will be the first to tell you that I did not become successful without help along the way. My experience had been that successful people love to help people.

2. Accept responsibility for your actions:

When you make a mistake or fail at something, own up to it. Take responsibility. The sooner the better. What you need to be doing is thinking of how to correct the problem. If you can't fix it or solve it, do something else or start something else. This can be looked at as experience.

3. Seek advice:

Do not be afraid to talk to other people about a failure. I know I am repeating myself. But it is important. What I do is look for someone who failed at something similar to my situation. I find out how they handled their failures. Also, talk to people in your field and ask questions about the problems they have had to deal with. You might even have to pay for advice or training on the situation. I am in constant contact with people in my field. You would be surprised at the help you can get just by asking for it. It's a two-way street. You also have to be able to give advice in return. I love bookstores. I will go into a bookstore and look for books on the subject I am struggling with and read some of it to find out if there is anything I can glean from it. Some bookstores might not like this, but they make it easy to read in the store. If the book is good, I will buy it. Make sure that you have a good library. When I had an organization, I always had a manual on how to handle objections. Acquire tapes and books on sales. Don't be afraid to seek advice.

4. Research new solutions:

When starting a project or business or even an adventure,

do your homework. Do your research. When I started years ago, we did not have the resources you have today. Use the local library. They have sections that have CDs and videos that you can see or listen to. I was in shock at what you can get from your local library. I never thought of the library until I was helping my son with a project, and he didn't have the Internet. He suggested we go to the library and get the information. So make sure you check out all resources available.

5. Take action now:

The biggest problem with people today is that they never take action. I always think of the phrase that a turtle never moves forward until he sticks his neck out. There is no difference in your situation. Keep in mind that we all have failures, but it is how you deal with them that is important. Look at a failure as a learning experience. We all have the ability to come back from a failure. If you look at some of the most successful people, they will be the first to tell you that failure is part of the process to success. We learn from our mistakes. So, talk less and take more actions.

6. Be thankful for what you have:

There's a saying they say the grass is always greener on the other side or at least we think that. What you don't realize is that you still have to water, mow, and weed the grass. What we need to do is to be thankful for what we have. I thank God all the time for my health, my family, and the ability to work doing what I love. If you look around and see what most people have to go through, you will see that you do not have it as bad as you think. So be thankful for what you have and be willing to give back to the community or friends and family.

7. Have the right attitude:

You cannot succeed without a good or positive attitude. In fact, I wrote a section on attitude.

Attitude, Attitude, Attitude!

This is one thing you will need to be successful in business and sales. If you are just starting your own business or starting a new career, you need attitude to survive. I can't stress this enough. Earl Nightingale wrote a book called *Lead the Field*. I loved this tape series and book. I suggest you should find materials written by Earl Nightingale. One of my mentors, Dan Vega, reads and reflects on Earl Nightingales work often. Dan suggested that I go back to my library and pull out Earl's book and reread it. I have had to get a new attitude because I had become complacent.

Chapter Seven

Thanks to Dan, I have a new attitude. We all have to take a good look at ourselves and reflect on our attitude. Dan says when people become very good in their profession, they tend to stop growing. They are the smartest people in the room, and what happens is they start to stagnate. In fact, I realized I lost a decade to just coasting on my laurels. This was not good. We all need to keep growing, or we will stagnate professionally. So attitude is important.

A good attitude helps us overcome fears. Now you do know what F.E.A.R. is, don't you? It is "false evidence appearing real." Sure, we all have worries and fears, but it is how we put them in the right perspective and deal with our worries or fears. Let's look at what Earl Nightingale wrote about worries: "Successful people are not without worries or problems. Problems are a part of living. Let me show you how much time we waste in worrying about the wrong problems. Here's a reliable estimate of the things people worry about: things that never happen, 40 percent; things over and past that can't be changed by all the worry in the world, 30 percent; needless worries about our health, 12 percent; petty miscellaneous worries, 10 percent; real legitimate worries, 8 percent. So in short, 92 percent of the average person's worries take up valuable time, cause painful stress and even mental anguish and are absolutely unnecessary." I love that. What we have to do is develop the right attitude.

From Trenches to Triumph...

Henry Ford said, "Whether you think you can, or you think you can't—you're right." So have the attitude that you can. Can't is a four letter word from now on and should be removed from your vocabulary.

I have to knock on doors when I set up dinner shows. It is not easy. Every day that I have to get in my car and go out is a struggle. As I am driving to the area I want to work, I have to keep telling myself that this is what I do and I am good at it. Then when I get there I usually drive around looking at the houses. I find it funny when I can look at a house and tell that it is not the type of home I want to knock on. I, sometimes, will look for houses for about half an hour, and then my attitude comes in. I tell myself if I don't start knocking on doors I need to go home and get a job. A job! This is my job! This is my company, and I will not quit. Then I start knocking on doors. Usually, I knock on only ten to fifteen doors, and I have enough salad appointments to cut salads with. I will usually book one or two dinners from these salad appointments. Yes, it is easy to just quit and go home. You have to keep your visions or dream in front of you. We all hate quitters, don't we? So don't become a quitter.

---

[2] Earl Nightingale. "The Fog of Worry." *http://www.nightingale.com/articles/the-fog-of-worry-only-8-of-worries-are-worth-it/* January 4, 2017

Chapter Seven

How do you develop a good attitude? You first have to find out what your desire is. Is it to be number one in your company; be a better husband, father or friend; or maybe you want to get out of debt. Whatever you desire is what will help you develop a good attitude. My desire was to own my own business. What is yours? Here are some steps to help you start developing a good strong attitude:

1. Pick your desire or passion.

2. Write it down.

3. Place it on your mirror so you can see it everyday.

4. Tell someone close to you who will support you, your target.

5. Say it to yourself every morning and every night.

6. Picture it in your mind that it is happening right now.

7. Talk and act like it has already happened.

8. Write down the actions to take or do to reach your target.

From Trenches to Triumph...

9. Never quit.

10. Nothing is impossible, the word itself says "I'm Possible."

It is up to you. You can ask for help. So quit wasting time and get started.

I think Earl Nightingale put it best. In fact, the following points really helped me develop the right attitude:

> Our environment, the world in which we live and work, is a mirror or our attitude and expectations. If we feel that our environment could stand some improvement, we can bring about that change for the better by improving our attitude. The world plays no favorites. It's impersonal. It doesn't care who succeeds or who fails. Nor does it care if we change. Our attitude toward life doesn't affect the world and the people in it nearly as much as it affects us.
>
> If you'll begin to develop and maintain an attitude that says "yes" to life and the world, you'll be amazed at the result and changes that happen. I remember

Chapter Seven

the old saying, "Smile and the world smiles at you, frown and the world frowns with you." It's up to you how you view life.

I. Your attitude at the beginning of a difficult task that, more than anything else, will bring about its successful outcome.

II. Your attitude toward others determines their attitudes toward you. We're all independent. The success we achieve in life will depend largely on how well we relate to others.

III. Before you can achieve the kind of life you want, you must think, act, talk, and conduct yourself in all your affairs as would the person you wish to become. Keep a mental picture of that person before you as often as you can during the day.

IV. Remember that the higher you go in any organization of value, the better the attitudes you'll find. And that a great attitude is not the result of success; success is the result of a great attitude.

From Trenches to Triumph...

> V. The deepest craving of the human being is for recognition and self-esteem to be needed, to feel important, to be recognized and appreciated. That includes our loved ones and everyone else with whom we come in contact during our days.

Don't waste valuable time talking about your problems with people who can't or won't help you solve them. This will not help you but add to your problem.

> "Never take advice from anyone more messed up than you." – Tom Hopkins

8. Give back

In the Bible, it says it is better to give than receive. Try it, and you will get far more back than you give. A side benefit is that you will feel better. It cannot always be a one-way street. It is a win/win situation. How do you give back? It's not just money or things, but your time, your resources, and your energy. Look for ways such as community service such as tutoring a young person on life or career. Working with local schools can bring good results. Use the tools you have to help someone else.

Points to Review:

1. **Without failure, you cannot learn and move forward.**

2. **Failure is a huge part of success.**

3. **Have a good attitude and overcome your fears.**

CHAPTER 8

Building a team

From Trenches to Triumph...

In this chapter, we will discuss how to build a team, how a team can affect your business, and how to manage and delegate a team. When you know what type of business you want or know how big or small of a business you want, then you can choose the right people for your team. I have been a part of both one-man operations and large. Each one has its benefits.

Becoming a business owner is the best way to reach your dreams quicker. Simple, right? But not always easy. There are some pitfalls. I think the rewards outweigh the time and effort you have to extend. My dream was to be my own boss and enjoy the rewards. This all started when I was selling peanuts. I felt that I could make the money without working for someone else. Of course, I did not realize how much time and effort it took to run and own a business. Still, my desire was to do it myself. My father, on the other hand, knew what was involved, and I don't think he wanted to spend the time and money. His brother, my uncle, had helped his son with the business. So I was not able to start my own peanut business at that time, but the desire to own my own business was planted then. I think in most cases the desire to be your own boss starts when you are young.

Let's look at the one-man operation or sole proprietor. I am at present a one-man company. I like it. There are benefits that I think are good for me. My ambition was to build a

Chapter Eight

large organization in the cookware industry. I became the number two dealership in the southeast region for a certain company. I then received a devastating setback. My wife of twenty-seven years was diagnosed with terminal cancer. I had two kids to take care of as well as the pressure of taking care of my dying wife. This was what finally altered me. Even though I had insurance, the doctor and hospital bills took all of my savings, and I had to sell my homes in South Carolina and Florida. One day, while my wife was in the hospital undergoing chemotherapy, the IRS put a lien on my assets and took all of my money from my bank account. I had been working with a CPA to settle with the IRS. This is where the right hand does not know what the left hand is doing. I had checks bounce all over the place, and I had never had a check bounce before. I called all of the companies and explained what had happened and not one of them charged me a fee. I was able to get that settled, and then shortly after, my wife died. I had to take a long look at what happened. All my work and time away from my family did not seem to make sense anymore. I lost my edge or desire. I think I no longer had the drive or ambition to start over. I quit and became a one-man operation with not as much pressure and more time for my family. In the process, I met my second wife and decided not to spend the time building a larger company. You have to have a strong desire and a lot of ambition to build a large successful company. On the other hand, there are benefits which I like. I have full control, good or bad. If anything goes wrong it's up to me to fix it. If things go right then it's the result of my effort, and I get to have the reward. What I do have is more time for my family. That's a personal choice. I am not saying it is good or bad. It is a tradeoff. I am also saying that the direction you choose is not right or wrong; just make sure that the price you pay for it is worth it.

You decide how much time to spend and where you want your company to go. It all depends on the business or service you choose. For example, if you are an artist, you paint it, you market it, and you build the name and value, and then you sell it. You are able to make all the profit. In my case, I own a distributorship of a product. I am able to buy the product, market it, build the value, sell the product, and then deliver the product. It sounds easy and simple. It's hard work. Well, it all depends on you. If you do the necessary things and do them well, then it can be a lot less challenging.

You have to decide. If you choose to be a one-man team, that's great. Once again, I would suggest that you talk to people who are self-employed or run their own business by themselves. The market is always changing. So stay ahead of the game so to speak. The sales business has changed so much since I became involved over thirty years ago. I still love the business and have learned to change with the times.

Chapter Eight

When I first started in the cookware industry, it was easy to book a dinner show. People were open to new ideas and knew more people. It was easy to have four or five couples in a dinner show. Over the years, it has changed. We are more of a transit society, and people are under a lot more pressure. Both parents have to work in most cases. They usually have to work different shifts and have different days off. The cookware industry had to change. This is not a bad thing, just different. The marketing is also different. I had to change with it or go out of business. Today, you can still do the dinner show and have two to four couples; it's just a little harder. What has not changed is that if you show your product to people and show the value, you are still able to sell the product. The closing ratio is still the same. When I started in the sales profession, the closing ratio was 30 percent. In other words, for every ten people you showed your product to, three people would purchase it. The better you are at showing your product the better the closing ration. My closing ratio usually stays above fifty percent. I am a professional. I learned my craft. The numbers are still there, you just have to put in the effort. I am not bragging; you too can have the same results I do if you are willing to learn and willing to work for it. I am no different than you. It all depends on your desire and effort.

What is your vision? Write it down and then make what I call a vision board. You have to keep your vision in front of you at all times to keep it alive.

Here are some guidelines to help you:

1. **Believe in yourself.** If you are going to hire or build a company, you have to believe that you are going to accomplish your vision. If you don't think you can, then how do you expect others to? I strongly suggest that you look back at all the things you have done and know that you are capable of doing the task or job. Even if you are just starting out, there is nothing wrong with believing in yourself and what you can accomplish.

2. **Believe in your product or service.** I have always looked for the best product. I would rather apologize for the price instead of apologizing for the quality of the product. The customer should have the benefits of a lifetime of quality and service, long after my commission is spent.

3. **Write down your vision.** Nothing will happen until it is written down. For some reason, your mind will start to react toward your vision. Your subconscious mind cannot tell the difference between facts or fiction. Your mind will act as if you are working toward your vision because that is what it has seen. This also works in your sleep because your mind never stops. Give

Chapter Eight

your mind something to work on, and the sooner you do this, the better your mind will be.

4. **Share it with your loved ones.** Use your support team to help your vision. There is nothing like a fan club. We all face setbacks, and you will be surprised how your support group will help you when you need it. I remember one night that my daughter became my support team. She was only sixteen years old. I was on my deck one night feeling so low, so sorry for myself. My wife had passed away only three months earlier, so there I was leaning on the rail, deep in my thoughts. My daughter came out on the deck and looked at me very seriously and said very bluntly, "Dad, get a life. Mom has passed away. Get over it. Where is my dad? The one who is always so strong." I looked at her and said, "I am the one who is supposed to build you up." What she said to me worked. So you never know who your support team will be.

5. **Plan your work, work your plan.** I know I keep saying the same things over and over, but it is important to have your direction written down and embedded in your mind. Let me ask you a question. Do you think that the winners of sporting events thought about the gold medal every week or so? Or,

do you think that they had to eat, breathe, and sleep their goal of a gold medal?

6. **Reward yourself and your support team (wife, family, or close friends).** You have to take care of yourself and reward yourself to keep your goal or vision alive. Don't forget your family or support group. They work just as hard for your goals as you do.

7. **Give excellent service.** My belief is that if you take care of your customers, they will take care of you.

8. **Give back to your community.** Community can become stronger only if people are involved in making it better. You can do this by helping with some of the problems. Volunteer to help your kids' school or the local organizations that help needy families. There are so many ways to help, so be creative about it.

9. **Be thankful for what you have.** I feel that this one ranks at the top. We have to be thankful for what we have. I know the law of attraction works better if you are grateful for everything you have.

Chapter Eight

Now if you want to build a team, then get ready to experience some of the best times of your life. Yes, there will be pitfalls, so learn to deal with that and go on. Building a team will result in building new relationships and friends that will be with you for years to come. I have made good friends in business, and you will too.

Before you build a team, you have to decide a few things such as how big of an organization do you want, where are you going to build this team, and what is your time table? There are a lot of things to consider, but let's start with these three things. First, how big do you want your company; five people, ten people, or fifty or more people? Let's say you want to have a company that employs over fifty people, what is the first question you should ask? Am I willing to put the time to pay the price for such an undertaking? Is there a big enough demand for my product to grow to a company with over a hundred people? If so, then what area will be the best to sell or service the customer? You may have to move in order to accomplish this. Whatever you decide is your choice. When you make your decision, don't look back, focus on your choice, and go for it. The rewards will come for you.

Let's say you want to build a small business of five to ten people. You have your product or service, you have your location, and you have the support of your family. You are

From Trenches to Triumph...

ready to begin. I recommend that you have a business plan in writing and fully understand what is involved. You can enlist the help of other people to help you write a business plan. The library has a lot of books on businesses. Find the books that are written by successful business owners. The business section in most bookstores is huge. It will take time to sift through them all. Try to look for businesses that are in line with yours. Then study them. I know it will not be easy, but it is necessary. It is better to learn this way then to constantly make mistakes. This will help you find success, and it is usually the smart way to reach your desired result. I look at it this way: if you don't have a business plan, you are like a ship without a rudder. There are even books to help you write a business plan. Here is a list of some of the things that will help keep you on track.

1. Have a business plan. If you don't know where you are going, don't expect others too either. You have to find someone who knows how to write a business plan for you. Remember this is a journey, so find a good road map. It will make the trip have fewer challenges.

2. Have a supportive team behind you. No man is an island, and this could not be more truthful than when you start a business. Even if you are only a one-man company, it helps to have a support

Chapter Eight

system. It could be your wife or husband, family members, or good friends who know you very well and want you to succeed. You can join business groups such as the chamber of commerce, business meeting groups, or networking groups.

3. Have the financial backing. You don't always have to have a lot of money when you start on your vision or goal, but you do need to have good credit or a way to borrow money. Today's society requires it. I strongly suggest that you have at least three to six month savings that could be used as a backup so you are not behind the eight ball so to speak. I have seen too many good sales people with potential fail because of not being able to pay their bills and have to move on. I got a loan from my wife's grandfather when I started one business and paid back every cent. Funny thing though, my wife's grandfather said I was the only person to every pay him back, and he did not have to ask for it either. Keep your integrity and always pay back loans.

4. Have a good CPA. This is extremely important. I know this from experience. The IRS is no one to mess with. They are willing to work with you so long as you are honest with them. I think all businesses have had their dealings with them.

5. Have two or more finance companies that will buy your paper. In other words, make sure that you don't have to rely on just one company. Each company goes through different guidelines, and each can become tight at times. You must have A credit companies and B credit companies. The reason is the credit ratings of your clients. This is also helpful when you are looking for the best payout. It might not sound like much, but one or two points add up over an entire year.

6. Have your company policy and training material in printed booklets. Far less problems arise when everything is in written form. All the rules and procedures are in front of the employees, and no excuses can be made that they did not know. It also covers you legally when you have to terminate an employee over rule violations.

7. Have your company advancement program in writing. You will have more problems with this one because everyone wants to know their pay and position in the company.

8. Have contracts for hiring with nondisclosure and non-complete clauses. The reason is to protect your

Chapter Eight

company from being used as a training company whereby employees learn from you and transfer your ideas to another company. Believe me, this happens. The standard time for an agreement like this is one year. It can be longer depending on the type of training and job.

9. Have a chain of command in place. Everyone has to know who his or her supervisor is from top to bottom so that each person knows whom to report to. This is also good for reporting problems. You report to the person that is directly above you when a problem arises. If the problem is not resolved, you then move up the chain of command to the next person in line. Never start from the top and work your way down.

There are more, but this will give you an idea of how to start thinking like a CEO or manager.

Now I recommend that you learn as much about your product or service as you can. In my business, I made sure that I knew enough so that when a problem came up, I knew what to do. Let me give you an example. When you are running a sales company or any company for that matter, you will find out that people take the road of least resistance. When I had a salesman whose sales were slipping, all I had

From Trenches to Triumph...

to do was pull him aside into the conference room and ask a few questions. I would look at my employee's weekly report card and see what actions he was taking. Then because we had a flip chart that he used in his presentation, I would ask him to show me his presentation. Nine out of ten times he was not covering the basics. If you do not know the basics yourself, then how can you correct the employee? If you are a contractor and you do not have an idea of how a roof is put on and what to look for, then you are at the mercy of your workers. Let me tell you, if they know this, they will take advantage of you. What this means to you is the loss of valuable time and money. I am not saying that you have to be an expert but that you just need a good knowledge of your product or service.

Picking your team and setting up the structure of your business can be challenging. I suggest that you talk to people who have experience in hiring and training. Most are willing to give you advice. I remember when Tom Hopkins said at a seminar, "Never take advice from someone more messed up than you are." In other words, don't ask people who have no business experience for advice. Go to a person that has experience.

I will share what I do when hiring. The first thing I look for is how they present themselves. Are they confidant? How

Chapter Eight

do they dress? I even try to see what they drive and how they take care of their car. Remember that in most cases, people take care of their cars just like they take care of everything else. I know what you are thinking; I have even ridden in the cars of some of the top salesmen and had to take a shower afterwards. Those are the exceptions, not the rules. Here are some guidelines, and I hope you study and apply them.

1. Attitude: look for a positive attitude.

2. Experience: ask questions on what they have accomplished.

3. Vision: Find out what their vision is because they will work for their vision; so if it is similar to yours, you have a winner.

4. Company loyalty: look at their work history.

5. Trustworthiness: Would you have them over for dinner? This is where you have to use your intuition.

You will have to work with these people. You will probably spend more time with them than your families, so pick them wisely.

From Trenches to Triumph...

You will have ups and downs. Accept it and deal with it. If it was too easy, everybody would be doing it and guess what? The pay would be just like an order taker, standard wage or low paying. What you want is to be honest and fair. Be honest in all of your business dealings. My father used to say, "You can never cheat an honest man."

Plan your work, work your plan. Expect to reach your goals and expect your people to help you reach them as well. Why did I say "expect" instead of "hope"? Let me give you an example. I am not sure if all of the details are accurate, but it will be close enough. There was a school teacher who had retired. She had been an excellent teacher. All of her students loved her. She had the brightest kids in her class. A year into her retirement, the school asked her to come back. Here's why, the grade averages dropped, and the students were not progressing very well. What they had done was take all the misfits, troublemakers, and seat fillers, and put them in one class. The school asked her to try to help these kids and gave her the names and numbers of each child. She was so excited because the IQ scores for these kids were high. She knew this was what she needed. These students were ones who she could work and excel with. The school told her that she might have trouble with these kids but to do the best she could. The school informed her that some had been in trouble and others just didn't care.

Chapter Eight

The first month or two, she had a few problems, but she was very good at her job. She was persistent. As the year went on, the students' grades improved. In fact, they scored higher than all the other students on their end-of-the-year tests. The school praised her and gave her an award. She said, "What did you expect? I had the kids with the highest IQ scores, so how could I not have good and excellent students?" The principal asked her what IQ scores she was talking about. She said, "The numbers you wrote next to their names on the first day." Turns out, those numbers were their locker numbers. They were all below average students. You get what you expect!

I heard that story on one of my cassette tapes. It has been years since I have listened to those tapes, but I never forget the stories. If you look back over your life, I bet that you have had something like that happen to you. So expect to be successful and expect your people to be successful, and they will be. If you have doubt, then they will have doubt.

Also, a good quality for employees to have is loyalty. Take notice of which employees take the time to do a good job and who will put in the extra mile. Take notice of the ones who will stay late and come in early to help the company accomplish its task or goal. I remember I had a salesman who was excellent at selling. The company made a lot of profit off him. Then his attitude changed. He became arrogant.

He started coming in late and wouldn't fully complete his paperwork. He started to complain that he brought in all the sales and felt that he deserved more money. We always had Monday morning meetings, and I waited until the right time to correct this problem. When the meeting started, of course, he was late. I locked the conference room so that he could not get in. He had to knock to get in. I said, "Excuse me" and went outside. I took him into my office and handed him his last check and told him to turn in his samples. He just looked at me. I told him that I didn't need his attitude and that I was not going to work with someone who was not a team player. I also told him that I could out sell and out work him any day of the week. I told him that he was setting a bad example and hurting the company. For those reasons, it was time for him to go. Needless to say, he was not a happy camper. When I went back into the conference room, I said, "I just let so and so go. So if anyone wants to be the next one, continue doing the things he had been doing, and I will let you go too." Ironically, we had one of our best weeks in a long time. I had to get rid of the cancer that was infecting my whole staff. You will have to determine if you have the same problem and nip it in the bud. You can also find good people who are worth the time. They might be hard to work with at first, but each person deserves a chance.

I was currently living in Florida and would drive up to Atlanta, Georgia, from time to time to help my business

Chapter Eight

associates train or just for some good association. There was a salesman who became one of the top salesmen. I asked Bob, "Where did you find such a good salesman?" He laughed and told me that the salesman came in the office and asked for a job. He didn't look like a salesman. In fact, no one wanted to work with him. His appearance and manner was not that presentable. His speech was poor, and he could use some help in other areas too. Bob took him under his wing and worked and worked with him. Finally, this young man came to believe in himself and became of the top salesmen in the company. He won a lot of awards. Never judge a book by its cover.

Then you will have one employee who will work his butt off and can't seem to cut it no matter how hard you try to help him. I had another salesman in Charlotte, North Carolina. He was such a nice guy. He had all the things he needed to succeed. I truly liked him. I very seldom misjudge when I hire someone, but this time I did. I guess I thought with my emotions and not with logic. He was very easy to work with and learned the presentation very well. I would guarantee my salesmen a certain amount of commission if they did ten dinners. The amount of commission was $1200. He did his ten dinners and never wrote his first order. In all my years of training, I had never trained someone who didn't write three to four orders out of ten presentations. He was just not teachable. I liked him, but I also had to let him go. It was hard to do, but in business, business is business.

From Trenches to Triumph...

Building a team or organization can be challenging, but rewarding. There were some good times, and I loved the time I had worked with people building a sales force. I will tell you from experience that you will get more excited when one of your students sells for the first time than the student will. It is so rewarding to think that you have taught someone to earn a good living in sales. I loved it. I have trained a lot of good salespeople and will never forget the memories we have. Enjoy the journey. Here is another way to help you start your program of success. First, you start with yourself. This will help you with your other goals or visions.

A good friend of mine, Dan Vega, has been working with me during the last year, and even though he is twenty years my younger, I have learned a lot from him. As I mentioned earlier in the book, he has been mentoring me and gave me permission to use one of his programs in this book. I felt that this would be a good place to add it. There are a lot of self-help programs out there, but as you will learn, very few will last the test of time. Look at the different types of weight loss programs. Yes, you can lose thirty pounds in a month, but what usually happens on those fad diets? You gain it right back and usually more, right? Look at the gyms or health spas; their number of memberships jump every January, and by March, they are empty again. The problem is we try to take on too much before we are ready to handle

Chapter Eight

it. For instance, you might need to lose fifty pounds, so you go on a diet and lose thirty pounds in two months. You feel great, and the boiled chicken becomes boring, and you begin missing all the chicken wings and beer with the guys. It becomes too much, and before you know it, you try just one and then two and so on. In thirty days, you are right back to where you started. What you need to do is start a program that is so easy anybody can do it. See, it's not the program that's the problem; it's sticking to it that is the problem. What you want to do is start a program that changes the way you think and act on a daily basis. From research, we know that it takes twenty-one days to change a habit. So whatever you plan to do, do it in twenty-one day increments. There are seventeen twenty-one day cycles in a year. What you have to do is to be concerned with only the next twenty-one days. Here is the plan Dan laid out.

Set a specific time to get up every morning. Take time to think about the time you want to start your day. Mine starts at 6:30 a.m. My wife's starts at 8:30 a.m. Now once you have set the time, you want to get up and start your day and don't change it. It now begins at 6:30 every morning if that is the time you pick. Remember this is a program that is easy to accomplish. Start these as soon as you get up.

Step 1. Read something special. I choose to read a scripture. Small and simple. No more.

Step 2. Go outside and thank God for a new day and take a deep breath of fresh air. Then I pray to God a heartfelt prayer. Become intimate with your Creator.

Step 3. Read some form of educational material that you can use in your daily life. Or listen to a CD on how to improve yourself or your business. I read part of the Bible and meditate on it for just a few minutes.

Step 4. Exercise. Now this is where this program is different. You start out by doing only five push-ups, five sit-ups, eight jumping jacks, and five deep knee bends. Yes, only five of each. No more, no less. Then walk for only ten minutes. That's it. I know, I know, you can do a lot more but not on this program. This will help you develop a habit. You just have to do this for twenty-one days. Is this attainable? Yes. It is the act of doing it every day that is the key. Remember in twenty-one days you will add only a small percent to the workout program. The next cycle will be six push-ups, six sit-ups, twelve jumping jacks, and six knee bends. Then you walk for twelve minutes. It becomes an easy habit and easy to do. So every twenty-one days, you add a small number to your program. Once it becomes a habit, it is not hard to stick to. It is a lifestyle change, and it's for life.

Chapter Eight

Step 5. Plan your day. This is the time to decide your schedule and plan of action for the day. You have to write down the actions needed for that day. Then number them according to the priority they need to be accomplished with the most important one first. If you list ten things and number those in order of importance, your mind will go to work. Some days you might be able to do all of them, and other days you can accomplish only a few of them. Put what needs to be done on the very next day and do the same thing that day.

Step 6. Work out your savings plan. For example, when Dan started my son on his savings plan, my son could put back only fifteen dollars a week. No more, no less. Then in three weeks he could bump it up to sixteen dollars and so on. You would not believe what you can save if you do it regularly. Fifteen dollars a week adds up to $780.00. If you do not count interest in ten years, you will have $7,800.00. In twenty years, you will have over $15,000. If you put it in something that pays interest, it adds up even more. Only one rule: do not touch your savings account. I repeat, do not touch your savings account. Why? Because once you do, it is so easy to rob it again. Notice I used the word rob. You are taking away the independent you in the future. Invest in yourself first.

Step 7. Make a vision board. This gives you a vivid picture or your vision or goal. I would suggest you take pictures of something you want, like a car for example. Go to the dealership and take a picture of you in your dream car. Put the picture on your vision board. Then take a picture of the house you want to live in. Do the same thing with your dream house and so on with your visions. Fill the vision board and look at it every chance you get. Picture yourself attaining the things on your vision board.

Step 8. Do it now.

In review, decide on what your vision and mission statement is for your company and approach it with hard work and determination. Believe in yourself and build a team to support you. Keep in mind that there are certain steps that prepare you for success. Be careful when picking your team. Learn from others the things that are required to build a strong and loyal team. Then plan your work and work your plan.

Chapter Eight

Points to Review:

1. Without a team, how big can your business grow?

2. Have a support system behind you. Cheerleaders!

3. Apologize for price instead of a lifetime of bad quality.

The last chapter!

Closing!

From Trenches to Triumph...

I put the information in this chapter last for two reasons. First, you need to have everything in place. You cannot put the cart before the horse. By that, I mean have your product, your flip chart if you use one, your office policies set in print, and your training manuals. Second, you must have a good presentation with good power statements. For example, when you make a power statement followed by a question, you want them to answer as if they already own the product. In the cookware business, I would ask, "Can you see yourself putting the food in the pan? Then by not having to stir or watch you pans, you will have more time with the children to help them with their homework, right?" This is where you can shine.

The difference between a salesman and a sales professional is closing. If you can't close, then you can't sell. It's that simple. Basically, most salesmen are order takers while professional salesmen are prepared, informed, and confident.

What you have to realize is that most people today are sophisticated. They know all the tricks and the answers. You have a choice: be a better salesman or allow them to be. I once heard that people are professional buyers, and you're a professional seller. So true! As soon as you realize that, then you are on your way to successful selling, or should I say professional selling?

The Last Chapter

I will let you in on a little secret. The secret to closing is ABC. Always be closing. Always be willing to close the sale. A person can't close sales, or seldom closes a sale, if he or she cannot help his or her customers or clients make a decision about the product. This person cannot overcome a simple objection and isn't a salesman but is a professional visitor. What company can survive with such an employee? The key to becoming a closing specialist is acquiring the correct habits, and by that, I mean to know at least five or six closing statements for your product. The more closing questions and decision-making questions, the more successful you become.

So the question is "Where do I get this knowledge?" By reading good sales books, attending seminars, and working with the top salespeople in your company. I would drive a thousand miles just to go on a sales call with someone who knew how to close and make a lot of sales. The results were well worth the effort. I was determined to be a professional salesman. The question is are you? Today you have a gold mine of education to pick from. What you have to do is search for the information that relates to your product or service. Start reading other sales help books to help glean a point or two. I used to tell my salesmen that the customers have their books on how to say "no" and you have to have better books on how to get more "yes" answers than they have.

From Trenches to Triumph...

Now here is a profound statement: There are no born doctors, lawyers, accountants, nurses, or salesmen. Each successful person has studied his or her craft, understood his or her profession, knows his or her customers' needs and wants, and built a presentation that meets the needs of his or her clients. Every day something changes, so the professional must be able to adapt.

There are steps to becoming a professional closer. I will share the concepts that I have been able to use.

1. **Attitude is very important.** The first thing you need to do is believe. I mean, truly believe that you will close sales. You are the best, and keep telling yourself that. I know it sounds crazy, but you need to believe it. The more you tell yourself this, the more you become a closer.

2. **Make sure your client or customer knows what you are selling or offering.** You would be surprised to know that most salespeople ask for the order long before it is time. What happens is they know the product so well that they think that the customer will understand it right off. This is not so. I always make my closes as if they are geared toward a twelve-year-old. Not that my customers are children, but when you are explaining something

they might not have heard before, they usually do not catch the meaning or value at first. I learned to explain everything at least three times and slow down to half speed when going over the offer and the price. Why? Because you are spending their money, not yours. Always keep your customer in mind. I always try to put myself in the customers' position and ask myself, "Would I buy this?" Also, one of the best ways to close is to make an offer that is a win/win. In other words, it benefits both you and the customer. In today's market, people know how to buy when there is value. I always offer more than they expect. I make them an offer they can't refuse. You have to create value. Learn all you can about your clients' needs and base your presentation on that.

3. **Create value.** I would enter a home knowing I had two hours to create a desire and need for my cookware or alarms or food sales. Right off, you have to start creating value. How do you do that? Questions, questions, and questions. Find out what the clients' needs are concerning your product. Once your customers realize that your product will save them time or money or labor, you have them. Now your job is to let them buy. The thing is to create a fear of loss. This has to be real. You have to

prove your statements to them. Don't lie to them. It will always come back on you. Honesty is the best policy. I know what my products will do, and I did my best to explain it to my customer. I know that once they got the concept, I will be able to close and shut up. Let them think and see the product in their home, office, or business.

4. **Learn how to use your language in a way that is easily understood.** Here's an example of how I am old school. When I needed a computer, I went to the computer store to buy a laptop. The first salesperson was so bad, I walked out. He told me what to buy and talked over my head. Since he was young, he thought that everybody knew the terms that he used. He did not ask one question as to what I needed. I was there to buy, and he was there to sell, but he could not sell to me. Why? His mind was on his commission and his needs. People want to buy, and they want to own. So learn to let them. I went back to the computer store the next day and talked to another salesperson, and guess what happened? I bought. Why? The salesperson asked what I needed and proceeded to explain the features in the computer that fit my needs. Then he asked more questions. Before I knew it, I bought one that was almost twice the value of the one I

The Last Chapter

was shown the previous day. This was because he showed the computer's value to me and how I would get more use out of it by not having to upgrade as soon. He would always ask a question and allow me to answer. When I wasn't sure, he went back over it and explained it until I understood. I am still using the laptop, and I am very happy with my choice. In reality, his choice to find out what I needed helped me make the right decision.

5. **Believe in your product.** I always sell quality products. You have to believe in your product. It will show in your presentation if you believe in it or not. I sold cookware, and one of the most common responses from my customers was, "You love what you do, and you believe in your product, don't you?" I can honestly say "yes" to both questions. If you don't believe in your product, then you can't expect the customer to.

6. **The last is very simple.** Know more than five closes. Keep trying to close until they tell you "yes" or ask you to stop. Just listen to their answers or objections. They are only letting you know that they need more information.

From Trenches to Triumph…

I know there are more steps, but these will help you get started on a good sales career.

Here are some points to remember.

- A. **Sell yourself first.**
- B. **Stay away from negative people.**
- C. **Know your product and your competition as well.**
- D. **Keep a positive attitude.**
- E. **Keep learning.**
- F. **Talk success.**

Learn what can hurt your sales as well. We all make mistakes. Accept it and go on. The best statement I have learned to say after I missed a sale is "Next!" Here are some things to think about:

1. **Don't talk too much.** Know when to shut up.
2. **Learn to listen.**

The Last Chapter

3. **Don't seem too desperate or eager.**

4. **Don't ever give a half-cocked presentation.** You are cheating yourself and your customer.

5. **Stay on your presentation** and do not allow it to drift into something else. Always keep the conversation geared toward your product's benefits and features.

6. **Practice, practice and then practice** some more. I still go over my presentation before I go on a sales call. You have to stay sharp. Remember people will buy from people who know the product and have their questions answered.

7. **Never stop reading or attending seminars in your field.**

I remember reading a book on closing, and it gave seven secrets to closing. I would like to share them with you.

1. Have no doubt. In other words, you close by assuming the customer is going to buy.

2. Use smaller choices that lead up to a sale. Such as, "What day would you expect delivery: Monday or Tuesday?" If they tell you, start writing up the sale.

3. I would always have my pen in my hand when explaining the offer. As soon as I ask the question, "Which one would fit your needs?" and customers choose, I would hand them the pen. If they took the pen, I knew it was time to write up the order.

4. Create urgency. We had a first call special. So if customers waited, they would lose out on my special offer. People hate to lose value.

5. Use third person stories. Talk about customers who love and use your products and service. Also, use real situations. Use real names whenever it is possible.

6. Use your specials to your advantage. We usually gave two items on the first call special. I would use the second to get referrals or another appointment.

7. After you have built value and your customer is ready to buy, do the most important thing: Ask for the order. You would be surprised at how many so-called salespeople never ask for the order. I was a sales trainer, and one of the biggest problems I noticed was very few salespeople asked for the order. They were afraid of the word "no." I would

The Last Chapter

always stop during my training to repeat "no" eight to ten times to them. Then I would ask them if it hurt them. When they said "No," I would say, "Of course, it didn't. You are going to get a lot of *no's*, so don't be afraid of the word." Sounds silly, but it works.

This chapter was for new and experienced salesmen. I know that in order to stay on top of your profession, it takes effort. Even though I sometimes go on automatic pilot, we all need to practice our craft. So enjoy your career.

I hope you have enjoyed what you have read so far. I have put in a lot of time and soul searching to write this book. In this chapter, I just want to summarize my book to help you get started with your vision.

First, think about who you are and where you came from. You too have a defining moment or two to reflect on. I hope it gave you character and integrity to work for your vision or goal. The thing to remember is that you control how it will affect you. Life is about choices. You can choose to be a winner, or you can choose to be a loser. You can even choose to do nothing, and something will happen. Your choices then are made by something else or an event.

Second, write down what you really want and desire. Make it a long list, and see yourself attaining those goals. Feel it. Taste it. Hear the praise of reaching your goals. Whatever you believe, you can achieve if you are willing to pay the price.

Third, put God first, then family, then business; and you cannot fail. Just keep them in that order, and so many problems can be worked through or solved. Love your family and never take them for granted. Have a passion for your business. I hope you have the support of your family.

Fourth, plan your work and work your plan. You have to know where you are going and how you are going to get there. Weigh the cost.

Fifth, build a support network. No man is an island. I learned that the hard way, but I did learn. Two heads are better than one.

Sixth, never stop educating yourself. Never, never, never! I can look back at my career and see the times I quit educating myself. Each time I quit educating myself, my income would always suffer. I like learning about my profession, and you should too and have a passion for it.

The Last Chapter

Seventh, enjoy the journey and share with others what you have learned. I find that I will help a salesman for no other reason than it feels good.

What you do now is up to you. You can put this book down and say, "I got a lot of advice with some nice stories" and forget about it, or you can start a new approach to your success. It is up to you. One of my mentors, Dan Vega, never stops learning. He is always reading, talking to people, and working on his craft. Success doesn't just happen. If you think so, then you are in for a lot of heartache.

I have A.D.D., so I jump around a lot and can't keep my mind focused on anything for very long. That's my story, and I'm sticking to it. All kidding aside, you have to know your weaknesses and learn to use them in your favor. I have a hard time working on one thing for any length of time, so I work on two or three things at a time. This gives me the opportunity to change projects and still be moving forward. Don't do too many projects at once because you will never finish anything. I guess that is why my book has taken me as long as it has finish.

Please don't stop learning or training your mind. I really believe that if you don't use it, you will lose it. I recommend that you find out who are the most successful in your chosen field and spend time with them. Most of them are delighted to offer advice or help you in your pursuit. I always did this. In fact, I remember when I first started in the cookware business. I was at a meeting in Greenville, South Carolina, and one of the speakers there, Bob, had the number one office at the time. Bob closed his speech with this statement, "If any of you would like to come by our office, we would be glad to share with you what we do, and answer any questions to help you in your business." This was one of my firsts meetings with that company, and I didn't know any of the people there except my trainer. As soon as the meeting ended, I approached Bob and asked, "Were you serious about anybody stopping by your office for help?" Bob's reply was, "Sure, just give us a call and set up a time so we will be able to set aside some time for you."

The very next day when I arrived home, I called Bob to ask if I could visit his office. Bob asked, "When?" and I said, "Now." Not only did Bob help me, but also the company bent over backwards to help me. They showed me everything they did and were very open. As a result, both of the owners and I became very good friends. To this day, we still share advice with one another. Never think that the big leaders will not help you.

A funny thing came out of this. I asked Bob if anyone else asked to come by his office. He said I was the only one. To make a long story short, they were the number one business

The Last Chapter

in the southeast region as well as the entire corporation. After all the help and advice they gave me, I became number two in the region. A few years later, we opened an office together, and it was very successful. You never know where things will end up. Take advantage of any help from the top producers.

I always took the advice or help anyone in my chosen field had to offer. Why? It cut out a lot of wasted time and effort. In return, I have always tried to help the new people in whatever company I am with. The thing I realized was that I usually benefited even more than the person I helped, and you will too. I don't mean money-wise but personally.

Closings

Other authors and sales professionals use several of these closings. One of my favorite trainers is Tom Hopkins. He practically invented the soft sale. I learned it, and it is the best technique I have ever used to this day. I strongly suggest you read his books and attend a seminar hosted by him. I met Tom at the Saddlebrook Resorts in the early 90's. I bought his tapes and went home and listened to them every day in my car for weeks. At that time, I had a closing ratio of forty percent to forty-five percent. Remember a good salesperson is considered good at thirty percent closing ratio. Although I was higher than that, I still wanted to be better. After learning his techniques, I jumped to over sixty-five percent closing ratio. To me, I had just made back my investment in his tapes (which was over $300.00 at the time). Ed just wrote a book with the title of "The Lost Art of Direct Sales." It is a great book for reviewing the process of sales. After reading the book, I had the opportunity to talk with him personally on the telephone, and he told me about his days as Tony Robbins' mentor. I hope to meet Tony in person in the near future.

Now let me explain what all the closes above are and how to institute them into your sales program. Let's start with the:

1. **Puppy close.** When you buy a pet for the family, you go to the local pet store or dog pound. They all look cute. You and the family pick one out, and the owner lets you take it home as a trial just overnight. It's your purpose to see how the kids follow instructions to make sure the pet is properly cared for. By the next morning, you can't see your family living without this new family member. It has become one of your own family members. Again, you did all the work for the salesperson. You sold to yourself. Once you sell to yourself, you own it. It works every time. This is also a great tool of the automobile sales industry. If you like the car,

The Last Chapter

the dealership will let you take it home for a few days, drive it, and see what you think. If you like it, then it will feel like it's yours. All that is left is the paperwork. This close appeals to all the senses. The leather or fabric seats are fresh and clean, so they smell good. It's comfortable, so much more than the old clunker you left at the dealership for collateral. All of your senses are heightened, and the car starts to make you feel good. You need this car. Now you start to justify your choice. As you are driving home, you think, "Who can I show my new car to?" A neighbor or a friend? Usually what happens is your neighbors will all gather around the car and start admiring it. Your wife takes it down the road, and more neighbors admire it. Hey, let's take the car down to the school and pick up the kids. Wow, the kids see it, and all their friends admire it and think, "Wow, his parents have a really nice car."" Sunday morning, you take it to church. More admirers. Everybody sees you sitting in it. Heck, by Monday morning, you own this car. You've done all the work for the salesman. You sold yourself a car, and there is no way you will leave the lot without your new car. Pride of ownership, right? I remember a time many years ago; if your TV broke, you would take it to a repairman. While he prepared your black and white TV, he gave you a color TV to use until

From Trenches to Triumph...

the repair was complete. Imagine, just what do you think would happen upon getting the call to pick up your black and white repaired TV in a few days after watching TV in color? You had all your friends over to watch their favorite shows in color. How can you return the loaner and go back to watching black and white TV? No way! The black and white TV went into the spare bedroom, and you purchased the color TV, which was just the way it had to be. Smart salesman. You did all the work, and he got the sale. I had this happen to me in my cookware business. I had a customer call me because he wanted to make a big turkey and needed a very large pan to cook it in. The set he purchased did not have a pan this size. I had a premium item that would fit the bill, but it was $350.00, and he didn't have the money at the time. I lent him the pan for his turkey dinner. When I picked the pan up, he purchased it from me because he couldn't live without it. What a hit! Who sold to him? He sold to himself!! I know a young couple who washes windows for a living. They go into small businesses and introduce themselves to the owners and give them a quick bid for the service. If the business owner is hesitant, they tell him that they will clean the windows for no charge once, and if the business owner likes their work, he or she has their bid for the job. Most business owners agree, have the windows cleaned, and call them back in a few weeks to set a schedule for the cleanings. If you are currently running a business similar to these, implement some of these suggestions to get immediate results.

2. **The Porcupine close.** You have to be careful with this one. You don't want to get the prospect upset. When customers say, "It costs too much," you simply look at them and say, "It costs too much!" What you are doing is throwing the objection back at the customers. Then it obligates them to explain why it costs too much. Remember the first objection is usually a smoke screen or the response of just a common objection the customers always use. In most cases, if they personally have to explain why the product is priced to high, they usually can't put it in words. So just continue on. If they ask, "Can I get it in green?" Ask them in return, "Do you want it in green?" They say, "Yes." Then you have your sale. If they say, "Can I get it by Friday?" You ask, "Do you want it by Friday?" If they say, "Yes," you have your sale. People sometimes ask questions just to give themselves time to think about the item. Once you have mastered this, you will use it often and be successful.

3. **The Ben Franklin close.** This is probably the easiest close you can use, and most salespeople don't use it. It is so simple and effective that we seem to not use it. You use it when you get down to the close, and clients just can't make up their mind. They want to buy it but are afraid to make a mistake. You must be very careful when you begin. Most have heard of Ben Franklin. Americans have considered him to be a very wise man. When he needed to make decisions, he developed a process to reach a right decision; you see, he wanted to avoid making a bad decision just like you. He would take a piece of paper and draw a line down the middle of the page. On one side, he would write the reasons to proceed and on the other side the reasons against proceeding. It's called the pros and the cons of the subject. If there were more pros, then he would continue with the decision, but if there were more cons, then he would decide against continuing the process. So why not try it? Begin by listing the benefits of your product or service and make sure you put down 10 to 15 benefits (sometime I read them) and then hand it to the clients to list what might be some benefits, with only one or two of your own benefits listed. Let them fill out the cons. They usually can list only three or four. Then look at the sheet and say, "Well, it looks like there are more reasons to

The Last Chapter

do this than not, so let's take care of the paperwork. Your address is?" This may seem old-fashioned, but it works. If there are more cons then pros, one of the reasons on the pro side might be so powerful it will overcome many on the con side such as the safety and well-being of the family, which is hard to put a price on. You want this process to sound natural. Remember, you are a problem solver. Your product or service will improve their life, making things easier for them. Reading the list out loud with them can help them make the decision.

4. **The takeaway close.** Once again, you must be very careful with this close. Smooth is what I call it. The object is to get to the point of the sale when the prospect is seconds away from agreeing to purchase, and you suddenly take the sale back. Yes, take it back. This works really good when the prospect wants the product but still fears committing. You now appeal to the prospect's ego. Let me explain. On one of my dinner shows with a couple whose money wasn't the issue, the husband didn't want to purchase, but the wife did. Finally, I looked at him and said, "I can appreciate that you are seriously thinking about our products, and I realize that not everyone can afford it, and I think this is probably one of those times. I am sure that sometime in the

future you might be able to afford it. I understand." I just shut up and looked at him. The silence is killer. I waited, not saying one word, just looking him in the eye. Moments passed. He spoke first, "I can afford this, and I can buy it right now if I want to." Then I said, "Let's make your lady happy and get this set delivered. I know that her happiness is more important than any amount of money you might have to spend." He replied, "You're right. I really want my wife to be happy and not have to work so hard, and the money is not an issue. Write it up." My wife was with me on this dinner, and she was amazed. The best part is that when I was leaving the home, the husband walked me to the door with his arm around my shoulder and said, "You know why I bought from you tonight?" I said, "No, sir." He said, "It was because you didn't put any pressure on me." I had spent almost two hours closing him and his wife, but because I did it in a way that was natural and low-profile selling, he felt no pressure to buy. I do this only when I know the customers really want it. They just needed more information and time to think. I gave it to them. I do not usually spend two hours. I feel that five to ten minutes is sufficient. You know you have done a good job when they feel it is their decision to purchase your products or services using these techniques. Practice, practice, practice is the only way to master these techniques. The better you get using them, the higher your income will climb.

5. **The Authority close.** Yes, this involves name-dropping. I use it all the time. If you are selling to a close-knit group of friends such as a church group, and the minister bought your product or service, let them know it when you do their presentation. You might want to say, "Yes, so and so, said the same thing when he purchased the other day." If you know their boss at work bought the product or service, by all means, mention his name. Creditability is what folks are looking for. Make it look like everyone is buying; no one likes to feel left out of a good deal. I am in the health and nutrition field, and I meet prominent people or experts in the field of health. Many times, they give me information I can use to justify the quality of my product. I research magazines, books, newspapers, and the Internet for pertinent information, and I make copies of these articles and carry them with me on my presentations and show them or refer to them in my presentations. Outside sources give credibility to what you are saying. If you have a high-profile customer, and he or she is willing to write a short letter regarding your product or service, have this

From Trenches to Triumph...

available for folks to read. Use every tool you have to solidify your product or service. A realtor told me how she overcame an objection when selling a home to a young couple. After seeing the home, the young couple said the home was perfect for them, but they wanted to talk to their father before signing the paperwork. The realtor asked a quick question, "Is your dad planning on living with you?" The young man looked at his wife and said, "Well no... we like the house. Why don't we go ahead and get it now?" The realtor's response was priceless. Quick comebacks are priceless. Practice some of them with a friend and learn to use what we call in the industry, third person stories. I was on a dinner show one time, and a young couple wanted my product but wanted to wait and pray over it. I asked them if they were serious about getting God's view of the matter, and they said, "Yes." Then I said, "Let me ask you a question. Do you think that God wants you to be healthy?" They said, "Yes." Then I asked, "Do you think he wants you to save money and not be greedy so you can take care of yourself and be able to contribute to his work?" They both said, "Yes." I asked one last question. "Do you think that God wants you to be able to provide healthy meals for your family and have more time to spend with each other and the kids instead of spending

The Last Chapter

time over a hot stove for hours and then having to spend more time cleaning up?" They said, "I am sure he does." Then I said, "Does it not make sense to go ahead and invest in this cookware because it does those very things: it saves you time in the kitchen, saves money in your budget, and promotes good health." They thought for a moment and said, "You're right. Let's go ahead and get it, and thank you for helping us make our decision." You see it was their decision. Again, the right questions and prodding will work.

6. **The Similar Situation close.** No matter what your service or product is, it is purchased for two reasons: it fulfills a need or a particular situation. Look at the type of people who have bought your product or service in the past. Evaluate the type of need or situation your product or service fulfilled for them. When you start prospecting, look for the same type of people. Think about it; in most cases, people are very much alike in their purchasing process to their neighbors or intimate friends. Birds of a feather flock together. I was doing my program for friends of a customer who had just invested in my cookware. Through the whole program, they asked the same questions as the previous customer, enjoyed the program, but when it came

to purchasing, they did not indicate an interest to invest. This baffled me. It took me a minute to remember their friends' investment, and it dawned on me that I had the same issues with their friends. So I started to ask them the same questions I had asked their friends who had just purchased. As I was packing up my cookware to leave, I asked them the following: "I know in the past you folks told me that you feel bad because you are always buying fast food for the kids. Are you still going to keep doing that now since you realize from my program that it is so harmful to their health? You know the Smiths were just like you guys during their dinner party. They too wanted to have healthy children like you do, but Mr. Smith decided that he should invest in the set because the health benefits for his kids were very important to him. I am sure you feel the same way. What I found is that most parents really felt that the health of their kids was very important, and I am sure you do too, am I right?" Then they bought! You see I put them in the same situation as their friends, and they saw the need to purchase. So let them make their decision to do the same as their friends. Now, do you think this was just a con tricking them into buying? No! In fact, both families are better off because they are saving not only their children's health but also their time and money. It

The Last Chapter

is a win/win situation. You have to work for them just as hard as you have to work for yourself. Listen to their needs. During your close, remind them what they told you, and they will invest because you are fulfilling a need. The longer you are in sales, the more experiences you will have. I have had so many I could write page after page of them. I enjoyed what Donald Trump said about Robert Kiyosake in Rich Dad Prophecy about experiences: "You cannot learn to swim from a textbook." He followed this statement with "You cannot learn business from a textbook or from business school." In other words, nothing can compare to frontline experience. I call it being in the trenches. Out in the field. Across the table. Face to face. Get the picture?

7. **"I want to think it over" close.** When often confronted with these words, you will learn to hate them. But you will have to deal with them. Remember what the warning kids receive from their parents is "don't sign anything." So they will use the phrase "I want to think about it." I have over the years spent more time overcoming this objection than any of the others. This is a very common objection, but I want you to be prepared to overcome it. What you need to determine first is the reason for the objection. Is it because they really

are not interested and want you to leave, or have you not given them enough information to make an educated purchase. This might be only a first line of defense for you to overcome. Sometimes when I am making a purchase, I will use this objection just to see if the individual I am dealing with is a real sales pro. How he or she handles it will be very important to whether I purchase from him or her. If he or she handles my objection like a professional, I will no doubt buy from him or her and even mentally record how he or she handled it and use it myself in the future. I will only buy products from a professional. If I am dealing with a salesperson and can tell that his or her only objective is to make a sale, then I will make him or her earn my business. I will explain him or her that because of this statement or that statement he or she just lost my business. Most salespeople are not properly trained. I usually take a few minutes to explain why he or she lost my business. Some have thanked me; others just want to get someone else in the store. The trick is to present a sense of urgency when I am selling a product or service I like. This can be done in a couple of different ways. For instance, if you are in real estate, and clients are taking a long time making a decision, you might want to remind them about some costly mistakes related to real estate such as interest rates. You could explain that interest rates vary and change daily. If they want a certain rate, it would be to their advantage to secure a loan while the rates are lower. Show them on paper how the rates can affect the loan payment over the life of the loan. If they like the home location, school, and price of the home, compare the cost of waiting and paying more for the home with the cost of locking in their rates and save over time possibly thousands of dollars. Put it into terms they can relate to. People hate to lose money, and they really hate a salesperson who doesn't present all scenarios so they can make an educated decision. I heard a statement a while back that has stuck with me. "People don't care about how much you know until they know how much you care." Practice using objections with friends so you are smooth and convincing. It's all about moving folks to make decisions for them.

8. **Reductions to the ridiculous close.** Car dealers are famous for this. They will sell you a car on payments not on retail price. If a car costs $25,000.00, this figure could overwhelm you. But if the dealer breaks it down into terms you can understand, it is more likely to be a sale. For instance,

From Trenches to Triumph...

Price: $25,000.00

Initial investment: $2,000.00

Budget Plan: $23,000.00

6% interest: five year plan

You would do the math with the clients and show them their daily cost. Then you will go over the features and benefits one by one: new versus used, warranties, mileage, etc. Then you ask, "If we are able to do all of this for you today, what day would you like to take delivery, today or tomorrow?" You can do this with any product.

Weekly payment: $103.41

Daily payment: $14.77

Find out what their monthly payment is on their trade in and then close this way:

"Mr. Jones, your monthly investment on your trade is $400.00, correct? I know you really like the new car." At this moment, explain all the added features

The Last Chapter

and benefits that the new cars has such as GPS system in the dash, six speakers in with a six disc CD player, and so on. At this point, you should break down the difference between the $444 and $400. I use only the dollar amount. Then you write down on a piece of paper the difference. You are now spending $13.29 a day to drive your current car which is over four years old and has over 60,000 miles on it. You need new tires, and I noticed that you have a scratch on the rear bumper. Remember at $14.77 a day, you subtract the difference. Now, Mr. Jones, for only one dollar and $0.48 more a day you can drive this brand new car with all new features. That's less than a cup a coffee. I know you can afford this. Think about what a set of tires cost these days, and the repair of your paint. I feel that just that alone would make up the difference of one dollar and $0.48, don't you? So, Mr. Jones, when do you want to take possession of your brand new car, right now? Or would you like me to wash it and fill it with a full tank of gas?" Then shut up and let him buy the car. He is not looking at the $444 monthly anymore but the $1.48 difference, and the set of tires he knows he is going to have to purchase.

9. **The Negative close.** This is similar to the take away close. You begin to close using a negative statement

such as, "Mr. Jones, this might be more than you can afford. Maybe I can show you something else in your price range." Now you need to know that he can afford the item or service you are offering. This will make him step up and defend the purchase. Ego and pride enter into the equation. This close is not for the timid. Sometimes, I hint that their credit might not be where it needs to be for the item. I suggest we check to see if they qualify first before going on. Prospects will speak up, and they will want to show you they can afford it, so now, you can go on to the paperwork phase. Just be careful with this one. You have to know when you can use this one.

10. **The Secondary Question close.** I really like this close a lot. From my experience, people tend to make little decisions quicker than bigger decisions. If you can break a big decision down into small decisions climaxing to a big decision, you will have a great deal of success. Let's say you have a lawn service company, so when you make a proposal to a potential customer, you need to break the service down to them. Let us then ask them a question such as, "Do you want me to start the job in the front yard so your neighbors can see your improvements, or

The Last Chapter

do you want me to start in the back yard?" Don't ask for the job; just assume you have the job. If you ask them outright to buy into your service, you open the opportunity for them to back off and say they need to think about it. This one you need to practice, but it is one of the best closes you can use. Here is another example. Let's say you were selling clothes at a men's store. You could use this statement, "Mr. Jones, which tie do you want with your suit, the red one or the black one?" When they answer the red one, say, "Great! Do you want to take the tie and suit today or pick them up after your suit is altered?" People make small choices that lead up to big ones. Once you have learned this one, you will use it without thinking about it. It will become second nature to you.

11. **The feel, felt, found close.** If you have come to the end of your presentation and you have not gotten a positive response, try this close. "Mr. and Mrs. Jones, I understand how you **feel**, and a lot of other people have **felt** the same way, but what I have **found** is that after they have used our product or service, they have never regretted it. In fact, they were able to save twice the cost. When do you want to start saving money, would tonight or tomorrow

be better?" I am making these closes simple so you can take each one and make it your own.

12. **You get what you pay for close.** This close incorporates the "third person story" process. For example, you can relate an experience from someone else or one of your own personal experiences. I tend to use one of my own. In any retail store, you can buy cookware that is inexpensive. Even dollar stores carry bargain cookware. What I sell is premium cookware. Waterless or water-free cookware is expensive. Everyone wants a bargain, and when they try to compare my cookware with a store-bought version, it just does not compare. There is a difference in quality and functionality. This requires that you justify the price. After relating this to my prospects, I ask them the question, "So Mr. and Mrs. Jones, I am sure you will agree that if you go ahead and invest in quality first you will not have to keep buying cookware for years to come. Don't you agree that if you buy good, you get good?"

These are the many closes that I have used over the years, and they have proved successful for me. Once you master them, they will be successful for you too. Hint: start out using four or five of them and let them become natural. The longer you are in sales; the more closing tips you will pick

The Last Chapter

up. Just take the time to use the ones that apply to your type of sales.

In closing, you have to continue your education. (I am still learning.) Take any classes or seminars that relate to your profession. I still look for new books that I think relate to sales or human behavior. I will promise you that if you apply yourself and keep educating yourself to your craft, you will become a professional.

So you too can come from Trenches to Triumph.

Points to Review:

1. **Find the need.**

2. **Create value**

3. **Know five closes and practice, practice, practice!**

A Special Thanks to My Mentors

JR. Cater was truly a mentor to me. When I started in the cookware business, he trained me. And through the years we became very good friends. We have worked together through out my entire cookware career. We have always had each others back. JR is one of the most creative salesman I know. We shared ideas all the time. We spent months developing a flip chart for our cookware business. We both still use that one today with very little changes. We have had so many experiences that I could write a book on just that.

We both have gone through bad times. His divorce, and my wife dying. We stuck together and helped each other. My wife got cancer and the support I got from him was great. I remember when Freddie, my wife, had her first operation. We had to go to Atlanta, Ga. We took my wife's car a Toyota Camery. I never though how rough it would be driving back to South Carolina in a small car. JR was in Atlanta at the same time visiting one of his offices in his region. In fact it was the office of Bob and Bill. We had stayed at there house the night before I took her to the hospital. We stopped by the office after we left the hospital to thank them for the support and JR was there. My wife was very sore and I knew she was not looking forward to the ride home. JR pulled me aside and said take my Cadillac home. It will be a lot more comfortable of a ride for her. And he was right.

I know that your mentors can become your best friends. So pick them wisely. When my wife got to the final stage of cancer before she died, I call JR. and told him I had to take time off to be with my wife he offered to run my office in Charlotte, NC. So while I spend the last days with my wife he worked at my office and took care of everything. When I got back to work after my wife died he would not take a dime for his support. That's when you learn who your friends are.

No matter who you are you need help when you start a business. It can come from family, friends, or new acquaintances. In my case I have to mention two people who really help me with the business end of the business. I had only worked a business that was easy to do as far as paperwork and office operations. You did the work and you got paid. I hired a few people but the office side was minimal. Then I started in the cookware business and things were about to change. I remember I went to a convention for a company in Greenville, S.C. I listened to all the speakers and was very encouraged. However, one speaker stood out, Robert Rodriquez. Robert and his partner Bill Chatman were the number one dealers for Saladmaster cookware. During his speech Robert offered to help anybody in the business if they needed it and all they had to do was ask.
When the meeting was over I went directly over to

From Trenches to Triumph...

Robert and ask "did you really mean what you said about helping anybody with their business?" He said yes. We talked for awhile and set up a meeting in their office for the next week. This convention is where I met Robert and Bill for the first time. For some reason we hit it off right from the start. I felt that they were genuine and honest.

The very next week I showed up at their office. I was welcomed with open arms. To my surprise they made me feel like I had known them forever. I thank them for the offering their help. I ask who else accepted their invitation. I could not believe it. The number one dealers who had built a company in a very short time and no one accepted their help or input.

Right from the start Robert brought me into the office and told his office manager to show me everything that they did to run their business. They supplied everything I needed to build a business. I spent two days their. They would not even let me stay in a motel. They had me stay in there home. To this day they have always opened their home to me.

I lived in central Florida at the time and I made several trips up to the Atlanta office. We became very good friends in the process. We ever worked together and became partners in the Charlotte N. C. office. They had the number one office in Atlanta and I had the number Two office in the Southeaster Region. I learned a lot working with these guys.

A Special Thanks To My Mentors

Like many good friends we did have our up's and down's. But the thing I remember the most was the way they treaded my first wife. Just as we got the Charlotte office up and running my wife, Freddie, became very ill. She ended up with cancer. Terminal cancer. We did not know it was terminal at the time. I was not told until the very end. This was in 1994,and 1995. The internet was not up and running like it is today. I did not even have a computer. So I only took the words of liere doctors. I regret not taking the time and looking up her type of cancer. Anyway I digress, after-her first operation, I was told by the doctors that everything went ok. I was not told she was terminal. I thought she was cured. We were able to go to a Saladmaster convention in Dallas in 1994. My wife was doing great, and had got her hair back and it was a beautiful grey. And very thick. She always had thick hair but this was full and looked great. Bob and Bill and Freddie went together to the convention. When we got their Bob and Bill said they were taking Freddie shopping. They treated her like a queen. They bought her a beautiful dress for the award banquet. Had her hair done, and she wanted to have it colored auburn. It turned out so beautiful. They even got her new shoes. The just made her feel so special. I think it was a way to show their love for her as a true friend. I will never forget what they did that.day. With all that was going on with her health, this meant a lot to her, and especially to me. So I will never forget what these two guys did for my wife. We thought she was cured and was looking forward to the future. Just a few months later I was finally told that she was terminal. Up until her death these guy treated my wife with dignity and respect. So I will never forget what they did. After my wife died I lost my drive to build the business and left the company. It was hard and difficult but through it all Bob and Bill have remained friends with me. I just want to thank them once again.

From Trenches to Triumph...

From Trenches to Triumph...

I want to thank my daughter and son for helping me with the editing, and my wife for supporting me in my quest to rise about the average.

I would like to dedicate this book to my family. To My wife, for believing in me. My daughter for helping with the editing, and my son.

www.ingramcontent.com/pod-product-compliance
Lightning Source LLC
Chambersburg PA
CBHW021127300426
44113CB00006B/321